Death: a love project

A guide to exploring the life in death
and finding the way together

Copyright © Annie Bolitho 2019

ISBN: 978-0-646-80362-3

All rights reserved.

Without limiting the rights under copyright above, no part of this publication shall be reproduced, stored in or introduced into a retrieval system or transmitted in any form or by any means (electronic, mechanical, photocopying, recording or otherwise), without the prior permission of both the copyright owner and publisher of this book.

First published in 2019 by Kinship Ritual
Updated in 2024

Editing, design and layout: Lorna Hendry
Printing: IngramSpark

A catalogue record for this book is available from the National Library of Australia

DEATH

a love project

A GUIDE TO EXPLORING
THE LIFE IN DEATH AND
FINDING THE WAY TOGETHER

ANNIE BOLITHO

Annie Bolitho invites us to pause over a future that we must all face and yet resist preparing for. Her gentle invitation is at turns reflective, creative and practical. Put on the kettle, make yourself comfortable, and enter into this wonderful invitation to engage with the death of your significant others as a love project.
Ilsa Hampton, CEO, Meaningful Ageing Australia

Ever since the Egyptians put honey into their tombs, there have been rituals to help us with the awesome mystery of death. This little book conveys what we can do as families and communities to have good rituals today.
Cedar Anderson, CEO, Flow Hive

Since the 1970s, the 'death care' industry has become overly sterilised and corporatised. Today too many people don't even value a goodbye ceremony, or taking time for grief, and ask for a 'No Service Cremation'. Annie's book is an excellent introduction to the movement back to a focus on the individual and community, and the importance of finding your own way to say a proper goodbye.
Nigel Davies, President, National Funeral Directors' Association

Death: a love project will help Australians looking for unique and empowering ways to celebrate the legacy of life. Annie Bolitho's book takes the reader on an inspiring journey of caring for each other in community … right up to the last breath.
Jessie Williams, CEO, The Groundswell Project

Death: a love project opens up all sorts of possibilities on an important topic, with wonderful examples and well-chosen references to other thinkers on the subject. It is vivid, powerful, contrarian, valuable, elegant, warm. Annie expresses things with a simplicity that is breathtaking.
Kath Walters, writer

I read this book in one sitting. Amazing how a book on death can be so life affirming
Noni

This is a very special book about death - inspiring, helpful and a great resource for anyone at this time of this great change in life.
Jill

Thanks to the wonderful advice in *Death: a love project* we siblings sat with my Dad's body through the afternoon and night after he died. It was wonderful.
Kath

Our family is a motley mob with a lifetime of messy moments! *Death: a love project* has helped us to get into agreement about a number of really important things we hadn't really considered before.
Raine

I received *Death: a love project* as a gift, three weeks after my mum died. You might think it strange to be reading about death after caring for a dying person, but for me it was perfect and I read it twice. It is so affirming of entering into the experience of death and dying.
Helen

Contents

Author's note		viii
Foreword		ix
Acknowledgements		xi
1	Introduction	1
2	The pause that death invites	5
3	Love projects	17
4	Talking about death and dying	26
5	Experience, kinship and suffering	31
6	Death as a matter of fact	38
7	Making your wishes clear	44
8	Consider your options	52
9	Dealing with uncertainty	57
10	Young people and death	64
11	Taking care of relationships	69
12	Coordination and planning	74
13	Meaningful rituals	78
14	Involving children	86
15	Service providers	90
16	Vigils and laying out	100
17	Burials and cremations	107
18	Coffins and shrouds	112
19	Natural burials	117
20	Environmental impacts	123
21	Imaginative visions	129
Resources		135

Author's note

In 2024, after 15 years' practice as an end of life companion and educator, I closed my practice at a gathering of clients, readers, family, friends and newcomers to the field.

This revised edition of *Death: a love project* includes some minor updates to the text and the list of resources.

Foreword

When my elderly mother, Marjorie, died recently, time stopped. My prior experience of death had taught me to pause and be still so I could feel the magnitude of the change in the order of things. Mum and I spent nearly three hours together after she died, before the funeral professionals took her body away. I will be forever grateful for that quiet time together.

This thoughtful and comprehensive guide to managing the loss of someone we love invites us to take the opportunity to slow down. It encourages us not to rush as we make the many decisions the world demands of us at such a time. It suggests we find the people and the rituals that will offer nurture and love for the living and the dead. Most importantly, it encourages us to pause in a busy world.

As someone with a recent experience of death and dying, my heartfelt recommendation to readers is to spend time with this book before someone dies. It will enrich, comfort and help you when the time comes.

Julie McCrossin AM, 2019
Journalist & broadcaster

Acknowledgements

This guide grows out of experiences in my family, communities and professional work. It draws together many people's stories and experiences. Thank you to everyone who has joined me in the exploration of this topic, in planning for end of life, conversations at Death Cafes, workshops and conferences, and in quiet one-to-one reflections.

Particular thanks to Janet and John Bolitho for encouraging me to write this book. Our joint experience at the time we were reaching adulthood gave me a strong motivation to do better with death. It's good to have found peace with that difficult time together. Thank you to Adrian Nelson for your generous trust in my intentions, and allowing Glenda Lindsay's story to take its place as a vital thread through the book.

I could never have written, edited and re-edited the guide without the support of friends who wanted it to reach an audience. Thank you Bobbi Allan, Nicky Coles, Kath Fisher, Jan Oliver and Kath Walters for patiently reading drafts and offering great suggestions. I'm very grateful to Lorna Hendry whose editorial assistance enabled the project to come to fruition. Thanks also to those who have encouraged me to complete the project: Jena Capes, Nick Capes, Jane Boag, Anne-Marie Power, Gai Longmuir, Enza Gandolfo, Deborah Zinn, Bonnie Bauld, Lina Patel, Cam Elliott, Lyn Carson, Catherine Kato, Charlie Ohle, Christie Love, Mitra Anderson Oliver, Delia Bradshaw, Julie Martindale, Tova Green, Hilde Knottenbelt, Jen Hutt, Farida Fleming, Sue Fielding, Jackie Yowell, Jay Chubb, Marion Cincotta, Jill Trevillian, Naomi Richards, Sue Andrews, Bill Standish, Linnet Hunter and Steve Rothfield.

I've long admired Julie McCrossin AM, as a broadcaster and community activist and I so appreciate her writing a foreword that brings the reader down to earth at the start. Thanks to those who gave permission to relate their experiences, and to those I quote: Joanna Macy and Elder Miriam Rose Baumann, or Ungunmerr. Thanks to Dr Roger Dargaville for taking cremation energy use figures and making sense of them.

Thank you to all those in networks and professional development contexts who have helped me to share, extend and enrich my perspectives on the topic of death and dying, grief and loss. The hospitable conversations held in Melbourne in 2012 and 2013 with Kathy McCormick, Pippa White, Sandy Mann, Nigel Davies, Joe Sehee, Juliette Armstrong Sehee, Annie Whitlocke, Pia Interlandi, Libby Maloney and others were a

Acknowledgements

wonderful opportunity to build relationship and a platform for advocacy. My experience in the US in 2014, getting to know members of the National Home Funeral Alliance, especially Jennifer Downs and Amy Cunningham, validated and enriched a community-focused view of death and funerals.

Thanks to Ruby Lohman for involving me in the creative work of Death Dinner Party. High fives to Grant Broadbent Smith, Sally Keegan and Ann Dillon for our unique collaboration on the 'Death Matters' workshop. Thank you Kathy McCormack, Victoria Spence and Priscilla Maxwell for getting together to run a death series at Woodford Folk Festival. I learned so much. Thanks to Karuna Hospice Service. Thank you to Jacqui Weatherill and Deb Ganderton from the Greater Metropolitan Cemeteries Trust. I'm particularly grateful to The GroundSwell Project and Meaningful Ageing Australia and their wonderful CEOs and staff for their energetic work to help Australians understand ageing and death as part of life, and for their support.

Thanks to the Geelong Library, Kathleen Syme Library and Community Centre, Hub Melbourne, OneRoof and Nest Coworking where I've worked on the book. Finally, a most appreciative bow to Ekai Korematsu Roshi and Jikishoan Zen Buddhist Community for the opportunity to transform through Buddhist learning, experience and cultivation.

Introduction

This guide is about life and death. You may already understand the importance of end-of-life arrangements. If you don't have much experience with death, perhaps you are starting to wonder about that time.

Maybe you have had someone close to you die and the experience has stayed with you. The funeral may have been fitting for that person … or not. Either way, you want to consider what makes for a good ending.

You may be looking ahead, for yourself or a relative or friend. You may be in the thick of it and want some guidance. Or you may simply have an interest in how families and communities navigate an important time in their lives, and do this well.

Death: a love project

I am a facilitator of funeral arrangements and a celebrant. I lead workshops about grief, loss and death. At these workshops, participants take it in turns to read lines of Miriam Rose Ungunmerr's *Dadirri* aloud.

When a relation dies we wait for a long time with the sorrow. We own our grief and allow it to heal slowly. We wait for the right time for our ceremonies and meetings. The right people must be present. Careful preparations must be made. We don't mind waiting because we want things to be done with care.

The group quietens. People become ready to listen to each other. The spirit and intent of these words never fail to move, inspire and influence me.

HOW TO USE THIS HANDBOOK

Death: a love project is a handbook to read or refer to as preparation for death and its associated rituals. It engages with the complexity and richness of understandings and feelings that commonly arise, as well as the practical demands around dying and death. It is not unusual to feel nervous about death and see it as an unwelcome time of crisis, but many people experience it as a time of wonder and transformation.

Introduction

Stories of innovation and change around death and end-of-life rituals now appear frequently in the media, highlighting that the more you know, the more options there are for how to 'do death'. For example, you are not legally required to use a funeral director. You may want to have more control over arrangements than is often the case, or you may want or need to plan an affordable funeral.

This guide is designed to allow you to come in at a point that is most appropriate for you. If you have to do a funeral immediately, go to chapter 12. Chapters 13–20 also address things that you will need or want to consider at that time. For example, meaningful rituals, in many and varied forms, can enable people to share and come to terms with the reality of death.

Chapters 2–5 are about larger themes that can help guide your thinking about the terrain of death and end-of-life rituals. Firstly, understanding that death calls for a different relationship to time. Taking a pause may not come easily, but when relationships are sensitive it is very valuable for everyone involved to take the time to talk, listen and clarify. There's also material on the value of setting a clear intention. Finally, this part explores what kin and kinship mean when we are suffering, and how companionship helps.

Chapters 6–8 talk about different approaches to death and end-of-life wishes. They can help set a direction for conversations, planning and clarity about funeral options.

Chapters 9–14 cover plans and conversations that will make a difference to family, friends and others who are affected by a death, including children and young people.

Chapters 15–20 are about practical arrangements, such as choice of coffin or shroud, burial or cremation and their impact on the environment.

Chapter 20 advocates for the enabling role of imagination in honouring a life.

Chapter 21 lists online resources and further reading.

2

The pause that death invites

When a family member or close friend dies, a great pause thrusts its way into ordinary life. Death demands that we stop getting on with things. It asks that we look within and express ourselves in ways that are practical as well as emotional. It is well worth slowing down, even if we don't appreciate this at the time.

Uncle Fletcher Roberts, a Bundjalang elder from Lismore, New South Wales, once questioned me about where I planned to die. He was old and he rarely left town in case he died while he was away. He asked if it bothered me that I wouldn't be in the same place as my parents. When I told him that my siblings and I had scattered our parents' ashes in our garden in Johannesburg and sold the property not long after, his look said, 'What were you thinking?'

'Onwards, ever onwards,' my mother had always said. There were no aphorisms about staying in one place or making sure that our ancestors were at peace. My family migrated to South Africa as Cornish miners and Birmingham traders. We were always looking forward – there was always something we needed to do. The notion of honouring one's ancestors was seen as primitive. We weren't like the 'African' people who might go home for days or weeks for a funeral.

When my parents died, we entered into transactions with a funeral director and went from there. After we collected the ashes, we stood by the birdbath in their garden and scattered them in the shadow of the quince tree. One by one, we left South Africa and our parents' cherished garden behind and moved to Australia. Getting on with it was important to us, and that trajectory stretched out ahead and became our pathway.

I tried to explain to Uncle Fletcher Roberts that we were an inexperienced and isolated suburban nuclear family. Ours was not a wilful ignorance. We were shocked, fearful and coping with something far outside our experience. But his look spoke of his sadness for me and my separation from my parents and those who went before them. He was a man of faith who knew where he would die and that he would return to Country.

There were no words for the difference in the way he understood time and the sense of time I took for granted.

How can we act with equanimity and appropriate knowledge in the face of death without slowing down to make sense of the situation?

SLOWING DOWN

All of us will die, but no-one knows exactly when or in what circumstances. Even if we are well prepared, there may be strong feelings and some disarray in our family or community. Many workplace awards only allow two days' compassionate leave. It's natural to want more time. As with any unfamiliar situation, taking the pressure off and slowing down helps us become more confident and able to act appropriately. Sometimes, having everyone sit down to talk at an important point in the process might only take an hour.

There's no need to rush. Rather than having the person who has died taken away promptly, because the only thing you can think of to do is call a funeral company, it is perfectly fine to hold off that call for as long as you need. This might be ten or fifteen minutes. It might be half an hour or an hour. It might even be half a day or a full day. If you plan to wait some days or more at home before the funeral, seek guidance from an end of life practitioner or a small, flexible family owned funeral company on different approaches, and what will work depending on the time period you have in mind.

When someone has died, there is no emergency. Nothing needs to happen immediately. This is the time to stay close if you feel you need that. This is the time when you can call family and friends who would want to be there.

Many people have suffered the consequences of getting a funeral wrong through hasty action. Even if your normal approach is to act quickly and take the most efficient path, you might want to reconsider in this instance. You may dislike the slowness of working things out with others, but this is the time for it. Instead of focusing on moving things along, allow everyone to slow down a little and make thoughtful contributions at their own pace. Multiple perspectives, skills, ideas and approaches will help craft an event that will leave warm memories you can all draw on later. The fulfilment of preparing the ceremony is all part of slowing down.

Country legend Lucinda Williams has a song that's worth a listen. 'Fancy Funeral' hammers out the misery that results from wasting money that could be better spent on the daily requirements of life. But the wrong funeral won't just waste money, it may waste materials through the purchase of unnecessarily grand or unsustainable products. Bringing people from interstate or overseas to attend an ineffective ritual also wastes a lot of time and money.

My own experiences have taught me that there is no way to count the guilt and regret that come from memories of empty platitudes that didn't reflect a friend or close family member's true nature. My mother's paltry ceremony was over in just twenty minutes. Without any explanation, her coffin disappeared silently on an automated conveyor belt. I knew then this was something I'd hate anyone else to go through. The companionship of an experienced companion or family friend, aunt or uncle would have made a huge difference to all of us. As it was, all l wanted was to forget the experience as soon as possible, and in that process I also forgot my mother.

TAKING TIME TO PAUSE

Sometimes, for reasons outside your control, you may need to pause.

> Neill and his family had to accept that their mother's body needed to go to the coroner. Although she had been growing older and frailer, she had not seen a doctor or home palliative service in the previous week, and in these circumstances no doctor could sign a death certificate. Yet, having that time was good. It gave the siblings a chance

Death: a love project

> to get together, discover things they hadn't known about their mother, prepare for the funeral and be close to their grieving father.

> Bobbi's father died while her sister and family were in Europe so they made the decision to delay the funeral for twelve days. 'We became familiar with his absence. We had time to find Dad's letters and poems, and have long conversations and reminisce. We and our partners shared meals. We had a big and very formal funeral to organise, as Dad was chief of a worldwide Scottish clan. Slowly and easily, the phone calls were all made, the lists were ticked off and the funeral took shape.'

> Heather comes from a large family and her mother Marjorie was the mainstay. When Marjorie died, one of her granddaughters had a baby coming, and it was late. The family wanted to give the young mother at least two weeks before holding the memorial ceremony. 'It meant we could take time on the details,' Heather said. 'I learned so much I hadn't known about Mum. My brother, who had been nervous about speaking, had time to write and then to practise. At the end of the ceremony, everyone congratulated us on how wonderful it was. We were all beaming with pride!'

If you don't realise that you can pause, you may be locked into holding a funeral within five days. With so much to organise and get ready in this short time, relationships can suffer. Everyone's circumstances are different and there is no proper way to act. Bear in mind the possibility that you can ease off and not go into action to organise the ceremony immediately. Pause and gather yourselves. In this time, immediately after the death, the course of the grieving process is often set. If you take the time to pause, you can create the conditions and occasions that will enable the reality of death to sink in gradually. The shock will subside and grieving can take its natural course.

GOING ON THE JOURNEY WITH GLENDA

My friend Glenda and I had a lot in common but, although she lived close by, we only saw each other from time to time. We'd book tickets to an unmissable concert or make a date to have lunch and admire each other's gardens. I often remember how mindfully she tore lettuce leaves for a salad and chopped avocado pips to go in the compost bucket.

Glenda glowed with health and the organic dishes she prepared were glorious. When she was diagnosed with cancer in her early fifties, I couldn't believe it. No-one could. Yet I wasn't surprised when she rang to talk about what she wanted when she died. She was a great supporter of my vision and had often heard me say that it is valuable to take the time to plan ahead.

Glenda looked at this time as an opportunity. Firstly, when she died she wanted there to be a pause, a time for people to come together, take in the reality of her death and experience good rituals. She trusted me to be there with her on the journey – whatever form it took – and asked me to be her companion. She wanted ours to be a professional arrangement and gave me permission to use her story to develop my work.

DEATH LITERACY

Westerners are increasingly realising how valuable it is to take a pause in our busy lives in order to learn, plan, prepare and make informed choices around death well before it arrives. We are becoming more death literate. Just as with low text literacy, low death literacy makes people vulnerable to unfair practices of funeral company products and services. We may buy products we don't need, or worse, miss out on our right to spend time with a family member after death.

My friend Katrina's children are in their early twenties – the same age I was when my parents died. They know exactly what their parents want. 'No way are you going to burn me,' says their dad. 'Don't forget I am not going to take up any space in this city with my decaying body,' says Katrina. Katrina laughs as she paints a picture of the family discussing death at the kitchen counter. Some kids and young adults learn about death through finding a dead bird or losing a family pet, but Katrina's kids know it's an event that will require them to make choices for someone they love.

Not everyone has a mother like Katrina who can make a tough topic hilarious. Many of us still find talking about death too scary. We aren't exposed to death as often as previous generations were. In turn, we don't talk about it very much. But just because there's a taboo around death doesn't mean there's no interest in it.

There's nothing like opening a closed door to bring out creativity and verve. Death Cafes, Death over Dinner, Death Dinner Parties, Dying to Know Day, Death over Drinks and performance events like Cafe Philosophique de la Mort all aim to ease the taboo. Attending these events means we're likely to be more informed when someone close is dying, or when we face that time ourselves.

I have facilitated 35 Death Cafes, an incredibly successful not-for-profit movement conceived and founded in the UK by Jon Underwood. Anyone can download a simple guide to holding a Death Cafe, which must feature tea and cake. The ones I have facilitated are just a few of more than 4,000 that have been held worldwide since 2011.

At every Death Cafe, even in a group of strangers, there is always someone who takes the plunge first. 'Let's face it, this is a death-denying culture,' says Hannah. 'I'm in my fifties and I've never seen a dead body.' The woman opposite her is upfront. 'I don't know what I don't know and that's why I've come.' There's a man who's learned from the unsatisfying experience of his father's funeral and wants to do things quite differently next time. An intense woman thinks of herself as an expert. Her strong views are gleaned from long nights online and haven't been tested by experience. I'm glad that some of the participants report back.

> 'I'd just like to let you know that my grandfather died at the age of 103 years and eight months. I'd attended a couple of the Death Cafe events you run well before his death, and I think it's in part thanks to those gatherings that I was able to have a prolonged vigil for him and take the time to organise things, including giving him his last ride in a very classy, vintage car. As his carer of almost nine years, it was necessary to give myself adequate time to do this and to grieve.' Lee

> 'Inspired by the time we had, I've begun writing my will, my intentions for my funeral and what I want done with my remains. It brought me a great sense of peace and comfort.' Clare

The pause that death invites

The American movement for death literacy goes under the banner of the National Home Funeral Alliance (NHFA) and promotes family-directed funerals. Families take charge of arrangements at the time of death, learn that it's not as difficult as they thought, and pass on their practical skills to others. Circumstances for ordinary people during and after the global financial crisis made funerals unaffordable. The social justice implications impelled a volunteer-run movement of educators and guides. I've been a member of NHFA since I first attended a conference in North Carolina. I was struck at once by the fact that the majority of members are women.

For a family-guided funeral like this, you may still want to have access to a funeral company for the legal paperwork and specialist equipment. You'll need to shop around smaller companies that consider this part of their remit. Most corporate chains are nervous about families taking an active role like this, and tend not to have the flexibility to work in this way.

Through taking part in events, anyone can learn more about the palliative, dying and after-death periods. Although almost all vital information and action steps can be found online, GroundSwell believes that people in communities can help each other.

'Lived experience is a powerful catalyst for action,' says death literacy advocate, Jessie Williams. 'For me, it was when I reflected on the experience of my son dying that I realised that the role of everyday people in helping me had been fundamental to my healing and growth.'

By changing our perceptions of death, we can learn to navigate palliative care services and communicate with funeral companies and cemeteries on our own terms.

> By appreciating the importance of slowing down and taking your time, you'll find it easier to work with others towards an outcome that pleases everyone. Rushed funerals are stressful and often waste the opportunity to reflect and choose well. Relationships and individuals can be very delicate at the time of death. There is great value in having conversations ahead of time about what you want in the case of your own death. This supports the people who survive you by ensuring that they won't have to devote time to figuring out your wishes or making difficult choices like deciding between burial and cremation.

Love projects

The title and much of the content of this book are drawn from my work and my experiences in my own family, communities and workplaces. We've spent the times of our lives together. Some of us have died. Some of those close to us have died. Sometimes the death was anticipated. Sometimes we were there, sometimes we weren't. News of a death often left us in shock.

People sometimes ask me how I got into this line of work. When I was twenty, my best friend died instantly in an accident with a semitrailer. The following year, I was in an accident where two young people and a large family died. None of my friends or family had any idea what to say or do to help me. At that time, my mother knew she would soon die from breast cancer, but we never talked about it as a family. My father was preoccupied with her illness and not well himself. He didn't survive my mother very long.

The concept of a love project came to me after hearing a story over lunch in a restaurant called Catinalla's. The restaurant was a loving tribute to the owner's mother-in-law, Catinalla. Later, in Glenda's household, I noticed love projects springing out of people's joint effort at a demanding time of sorrow and suffering, uncertainty, joy, longing, frustration and warmth. Now that the concept of a love project is embedded in my practice, I hear about them all the time.

My experience has been that a healing love project can begin years after a traumatic experience of death. Without knowing how, I wanted to use my experience to benefit others and I made a commitment to do so. Without knowing how, I wanted to be able to talk and grieve with my brother and sister and their children.

In my workshops and Death Cafes, stories bring to light how our experiences of working it out along the way when someone is dying can linger. There are nurturing memories and a sense of it all having been worthwhile and enlightening. Some friends and families find wonderful ways of taking the contribution of a loved one forward, as Catinalla's daughter-in-law did. There are also stories of people shutting down, being isolated, hostile, hesitant to act and deeply fearful.

How can this be helped? What value judgements about time, relationships, life and death get in the way of being together respectfully at an important time and doing the best we can? What impedes the natural course of grieving?

The answer does not lie with experts. When embarking on a love project, we encounter uncertainties rather than answers. Relationships are sensitive in the face of loss. Different perspectives jostle for our attention and all need to be taken into account. Having an understanding of the practical choices and decisions helps, perhaps more than anything else, to take care of the feelings that surge forward with loss. Tackling these tasks well doesn't just help at the time of the death, but continues into the future.

EMBRACING FEAR AND GRIEF

Michael Leunig once wrote that love and fear are ruling elements in how we live our lives. Fear is okay. Acknowledging it is a good place to start looking at death. Given some attention and care, fear will pass. It will arise again but, treated gently, will pass once more.

Embracing fear is easier said than done but I often see people preparing for death, delivering eulogies and sharing untold grief in the most generous spirit. Quite a few people seem to have the capacity to meet very difficult challenges and simply do things, one thing after the other. I've heard people say, without thinking of it as anything special, that what they want more than anything is not to be relieved of their own pain, but to ease others' pain or lessen their fear.

In my experience, death invites us to act in all sorts of ways. During the time between the last stages of illness, death, a funeral ceremony and the unfolding of the legacy of a person's life, many people make a contribution. The sheer number of things that need to be done when someone close is ill, around a death, in preparation for end-of-life rituals and in supporting others through grief and loss is extraordinary. To me, the service and creativity of partners, family, friends and palliative services is very moving. For all the natural fears, frustrations and stress, people find a way through this time and mostly get through the hard stuff.

There may be many tears shed in the course of a love project. There is little hope of addressing taboos around death in Australia without confronting the fear of expressing feelings in public and having swollen eyes and a puffy face for a while. When it's unacceptable to cry out loud in front of others, or sob and howl when someone close has died, as is common in many migrant cultures, the full experience of death is deflected or pushed aside. When it's too upsetting to have a coffin at the ceremony – a growing proportion of funerals are held without one – there's a misunderstanding of the role of grief in navigating inconceivable change. It's hard, but it could be worth allowing the presence of a coffin – a powerful signifier of death – and having a cry with others.

CREATING A LOVE PROJECT

My friend Bobbi knew she would not be able to attend Glenda's end-of-life celebration or see her before she died. She lived too far away and had family commitments. Bobbi set aside a morning to look at photos, recall memories and write an important letter. She made sure that she left nothing unsaid about what she loved about their friendship and Glenda's unique contribution. This small love project meant a lot to Glenda and her partner. When Glenda's energy ebbed, she read Bobbi's letter often.

At its best, the work of taking care of end-of-life arrangements is a special and respectful process, marked by warmth, needs, aspirations, difficulties, contradictions, joy, suffering and care. It is a time when we enlarge our view of the person and ourselves. We might get in deeper than we are ready for, but this will stand us in great stead in the future.

Death: a love project

If the person hasn't given any indication of the kind of funeral they would like, it's a time to pause, work out what to do together and enjoy the satisfaction of doing it well. Even if you are still disappointed by the limitations of love and care from that person, it's worth reflecting on those qualities that you respect and appreciate as you plan.

> At the funeral, held in the local hall, the proteas came from Alison's garden, the banksias and bougainvillea came from Colleen's and the camellias and grevilleas came from Zoe. Zoe laid out generous spreads of greenery and flowers and made arrangements for vases at the front of the stage. This is a love project.

> John said of his mother, 'Judy is an artist before being a mother, before being a wife, before anything else … that's what makes her life flower.' When Judy was frail, mother and son held the John & Judy Show, an exhibition of her paintings and his sculpture. This is a love project.

> Lyndee and Mark discussed everything before he died. He said he knew how much she must be looking forward to getting rid of the workbench that had taken up so much room in the garage, and that she'd once reversed into. He told her that their time together had been rich and complete, and that if she met the right person she should repartner. This is a love project.

> Kristian, a sound engineer, had to undergo expensive treatment for cancer. When his need was put out to the music world, audio engineers and musicians around Australia donated over $5,000 in a week. Only a few of the donors had ever met him. This is a love project.

A few years ago I read this warm account by Joanna Macy describing how her family and friends were with her when her husband died.

Given the shock and suddenness of it all, it made a huge difference to bring Fran's body home.

It was a surreal and exquisite night. Our bedroom filled with flowers, candlelight, music – Russian liturgies and Bach cello suites. With scented water and rose petals in a Palestinian bowl he'd given me for Christmas, Fran's beautiful body was washed slowly, caressingly, reverently by his son, his daughter, and his wife. Then we dressed him, choosing sweatpants and a faded denim shirt I loved, and tucked bags of dry ice under his neck and back and sides, and covered his legs and torso with a sheet of royal blue. He looked calm, handsome, and noble, like a Viking chief on his funeral boat.

The next two days, from ten in the morning till ten at night, people came to pay their respects. No idea how many came, all told, in that steady flow of friends and neighbours, some returning more than once. No need to ring or knock, just come in and up the stairs. Go straight ahead to the bedroom and sit in silent meditation with Fran, or read to him, or join in a song. Or turn right into the dining room where more bounteous food appears by the minute or join in a quiet chat at the kitchen table. Or turn left into the living room and sit down to draw messages or pictures on the muslin to be appliquéd to Fran's shroud. The sewing of that was in Peggy's domain downstairs – two friends took turns stitching long strips from her quilting fabrics, while the grandchildren and their friends kibitzed, choosing colors and making more decorations for Opa. What struck me above all was the atmosphere that reigned. I can still almost feel it, the softness and buoyancy of the air, a sweet lightness around us and inside us.

This is a family and community love project.

Love projects

It's possible to change the idea that death is a terrible crisis, and instead work together on what needs to be done in the spirit of a love project. Beneath the overwhelming decisions and exhaustion, and later the phone calls and the strangeness of being part of an unfamiliar scenario in which our loved one is absent, we will be better placed to wrap up the life in a way that is good, beautiful and true. All families and communities can do this by appreciating the importance of time and relationships and companionship.

At the heart of death is the mystery of life and human kinship, the possibility of strengthening family and community ties and of coming forth as well-lived people, who can make good, adaptive choices for the end of our lives.

Talking about death and dying

People can be very frightened of using the words 'die' or 'death' in conversation, but people who are dying usually know they are. Saying these words out loud can be difficult, but it can help initiate a frank dialogue about exactly what's wanted when end-of-life arrangements or a funeral need to be discussed. Death disrupts familiarity and the unstated rules and understandings that go with it.

When I help people prepare for a funeral or a vigil, I have two ordinary words in mind: 'family' and 'familiar'. Both words come from the same root. Each conveys intimacy and a sense of being well-known. When faced with the absence anticipated by or left after death, everyone feels odd. The household is not as it was before. Lineages may be up in the air. Familiar possessions become 'property'.

THE REASSURING ROLE OF A COMPANION

For those experiencing loss at the time of a death, it can be a confusing and busy time. A third-party companion who is independent of intimates, family or friends can help, as well as ease decision-making burdens. A dedicated friend or family member may do the same. This can be very useful if time is short and you need to clarify issues, make choices or get together for discussions.

If you are planning to do quite a bit yourself, do as much as is reasonable and comfortable, but delegate the rest to someone not intimately involved. Otherwise you might only realise later on that you took no time to experience the grief or the goodbye.

The stream of deaths in my family and friendship networks in my twenties, and being alongside friends over the years, made me want to companion others. When someone engages me as their companion to consider their end-of-life plans, our first meeting begins with a cuppa while I sit and let them talk.

I can make this difficult time easier through my experience with death and grieving, and my knowledge of cemeteries, shrouds, ceremonies and practical matters that are necessary but unfamiliar to many people.

Some people approach me because they've walked away from an important funeral in the past feeling unsatisfied or because they are burnt out by organising amidst grief. They want to have time and space to experience their feelings. If there are only three, four or five days available, third-party support can be helpful and slow things down so that everyone is heard.

A companion will give the assurance that there's no template that needs to be followed, and encourage imagination and creativity. They can bring people together to create an occasion that looks and feels joyful and leaves people feeling good afterwards, even when they are very sad.

THE POWER OF STORIES

As I was going to my car after conducting a funeral recently, a group of guests having a smoke by the open door of a ute called out. 'Thanks so much, that was great!' The fabulous, non-conformist ceremony was organised by friends and family. A child opened the proceedings, a poet strode in enunciating his response to the woman's death and her hairdresser did the catering. It made perfect sense to her friends from all the different parts of her life. But shaping these arrangements had taken time.

At my first meeting with a family there's sometimes silence and a feeling of anxious uncertainty, along with palpable sadness, around the table. How can we ease this tension and find a way to talk?

For me, it's almost always through story. Stories that come from experience have a credibility that outshines strong opinions. A story can give life to uncertain plans. People start to feel more alive and connected when they tap into memories, feelings and much-loved music. The unique perspectives each person offers light the others up. Suddenly everyone understands where the discussion is going. Ideas join up and become something no-one considered before.

FINDING AN AGREED DIRECTION

When someone is dying, familiar patterns of life are disrupted. The overwhelming waves of feeling that mark bereavement come at a time when important decisions need to be made. Taking charge may be necessary, but the person who steps forward to take the lead may appear bossy. It can be very confusing.

A facilitated family meeting with a third party can release energy for ideas and creativity. 'Wouldn't that song be the perfect opening? But what about that other one he loved? I'm sure I can find the exact recording.' A story begins to grow around what the end-of-life plan or the celebration of life could be. A eulogy takes form. Visual material is collected. Tasks get done. Good feelings breed new possibilities that are perfect.

> A companion who has cultivated the capacity to be available can help bring some comfort in a time of disruption by assisting with creating an inclusive, evenly paced process. They can give family and friends confidence that they will create a unique gathering and ritual.

Experience, kinship and suffering

Kinship is an acknowledgment of a shared human experience and gives a support structure through suffering and aloneness. We're in this together. Affinity, sympathy and the desire to be together make grief easier to bear.

I've had many coffees and run events at Kinfolk Cafe in Melbourne's Donkey Wheel House, a social enterprise near Southern Cross Station. The founders started out by combining a cosy aesthetic with an ethic based on generosity. In their business model, kitchen and wait staff who work elsewhere in Melbourne's thriving hospitality sector volunteer their time each week for a number of shifts at Kinfolk. Kinfolk donates all of its profits to charity.

Death: a love project

There is a real hunger for connectedness and community today. An underlying yearning to do things consciously and artfully has brought 'kin' words into our culture. My work goes under the name *Kinship Ritual*. The name came about from talking with a friend about what it's like being alone with thoughts, ideas and feeling going round and round. Being able to bounce ideas and possibilities off someone else can make the world of difference. Kinship makes working out plans for end of life a lot less lonely. Kinship creates companionship.

> In a Buddhist parable, a young woman's only child dies. She can't accept what has happened. Holding her child's body close, she looks for something to revive the little one. Finding nothing, she goes to the Buddha to beg for medicine. The Buddha tells her to seek out a handful of mustard seed from a household where no-one had died. Holding the child, the woman sets off. When she returns, a very long time later, she has laid the child to rest in a forest. The Buddha asks if she has brought the mustard seed. 'No,' she says. She has been changed by her encounters at home after home around the town. Buddha's gentle suggestion led a distraught mother to find out for herself about the deep kinship of being human and facing death and loss. Her enquiries would have given her community a way of expressing their kindness and compassion as well.

Experience, kinship and suffering

Kinship is still very much associated with anthropology and non-Western cultures – the kind of world Uncle Fletcher Roberts showed me, where an individual has no doubt about being interwoven with place and has long-held cultural practices to act on. Many Australians who are Muslim, Greek, Italian and Jewish know what to do around death. The rituals in their traditions are quite clear. This isn't the case for many Anglo-Australians.

GLENDA'S VISION

Needing some time to pause before I met with Glenda and her partner, I wrote this diary entry at Kinfolk Cafe.

> *This morning I've been thinking of Glenda. I'm so sad now the prognosis is clear. Where yesterday I could only think of her inspiring influence and how much she's taught me about making things grow, today it's different. The image of her held by her family on Facebook is right there in my mind's eye.*
> *How will we live without her?*
>
> *Haruki Marukami says: 'People are awkward creatures. A lot more awkward than you seem to realise.' I've felt so awkward today.*
>
> *I cut out a piece by the poet Pablo Neruda not long after I came to Australia, where he spoke words that comforted me.*

Death: a love project

'We must pass through solitude and difficulty, isolation and silence,' he said, 'in order to reach forth to the enchanted place where we can dance our clumsy dance and sing our sorrowful song ...' I've become so at home as an Australian, made wonderful friends like Glenda.

It's such a jolt. Now we know. She is going to die.

When there's all the evidence of physical and mental difficulty, denial only adds to it. Awkwardness is okay. In our awkward dance or song, Neruda reminds me, something is fulfilled: 'an ancient rite of our conscience, in the awareness of being human'.

Earlier I felt down, uninspired, not good enough, tired and as if nothing could help. And here I am at this place of contemporary community, Kinfolk Cafe. Just now the woman serving looked so directly at me. How can I help you? I immediately felt better. Even before giving my order. I felt alive. It will all be okay. I didn't expect to feel this change of mood.

Is this what kinship is? A face-to-face meeting. Attentiveness. Recognition that we're all human.

The kinship, not of blood ties, but of sharing a simple experience of exchange. Knowing beneath the level of consciousness, a fundamental closeness of each of us having four limbs, eyes, ears, nose, tongue and mind. The fellow feeling of having needs and wanting them met. Somehow this time, it was more than just a coffee.

Later that day, we sat around Glenda's table. With some trepidation in the air, we got ready to approach details of her end-of-life plans. She was very thin but still full of the determination that saw her inspire pioneering urban food projects in the inner suburbs. She spoke quietly about her vision. She wanted her death to contribute to lessening others' fears. That was the main thing. Then she referred to the points she'd written in her notebook. It wouldn't be a funeral – her birthday was around the corner so it would be a birthday celebration. Both the choirs she was involved in would sing. She had written their playlists.

She put her questions about the vigil. How long would it last? What would we need?

'It will be confronting,' her husband said. And he'd do everything to enable her wish to have the vigil. 'Thinking back on it,' he said suddenly, 'when I was young in England, people were often laid out in the front room. Should we use the front room, darling?'

I showed them the photo of the coffin I'd had made. It was a colourful box crafted out of fruit crates. We all laughed. It was perfect. Very Glenda! We didn't say a lot. But we understood that we were in it together, this thing of life. I went away feeling our kinship alive in me.

SHARING EXPERIENCES

Death: a love project

Over the years, I've held many workshops about death and Death Cafes at venues like Kinfolk Cafe and Nest Coworking. At the start, we're all strangers sizing each other up. But later we smile and laugh when someone says, 'I can't help it. I know other people might die, but it's not going to happen to me!'

We all want to make sure we say 'I love you' more often. We know what it is to take our mother for granted. When someone is brave enough to talk of a very sad time, a couple of people cry. When someone says, 'I feel a resonance with what you said', I know they're about to build on and extend the conversation.

At the end, when I ask people to write a word or two about how it's been, there's always someone who chooses '*connected*'. Then there's '*unpredictable*' and '*use the D-word*' and '*no-one will ever be an expert*' and '*celebrate life*' and '*weave art into grieving*'.

Kinship is a wellspring that people draw from. No-one leaves feeling miserable. They express their appreciation and say they feel enriched.

Experience, kinship and suffering

> In the face of the reality of death and loss, life feels precious and rich. Being in touch with the finite nature of life creates a sense of opportunity, even though it is very sad. Knowing about different approaches to death and having conversations ahead of time can make a real difference. Ritual can play a vital role in enhancing kinship among family, friends and people who aren't known to each other. Each person brings a different perspective, having known the person who has died in different contexts or eras.

Death as a matter of fact

Clinical treatments and the familial and social aspects of care both need consideration when you are faced with the fact that you or someone you love is dying. It takes a community and a network of dependable relationships to die at home. It's a time of adjustment, which can be awkward. At first, family and friends may feel ill at ease with talking and not knowing what to do. We can get very churned up trying to do 'the right thing'.

Since my mother died, treatments for cancer have improved so much that people's lives are often extended for quite a long time. This means that the subject of death is very often scrutinised from a clinical perspective. There is great reliance on clinicians in relation to life expectancy after a treatment or when clinical treatment is no longer effective. Hospitals and doctors are experts in keeping life going, and one clinical treatment often follows another. Although a high proportion of people wish to die at home surrounded by familiar comforts, most still die in hospital.

One of the great fears of approaching death is of pain. Home palliative care services take care of this. Still, it takes companionship and a network of dependable relationships to die at home. Everyone will be in touch to keep an eye on things and take the pressure off the main carer. Someone might come and just sit with their friend for a while. They might take the broom off its hook and sweep the kitchen, move a pot plant so it can be seen from indoors, trim the daisy heads or put on the laundry. Undertaking a love project, people find ways of doing their bit and negotiating decisions around care.

A SPECIAL PLACE

Karuna Hospice Service in Brisbane has been my charity of choice for years. Along with the purely clinical services of home palliative care, it offers biography writing, conversations and family events. In 2016, I learned that they were caring for a writer I admired, Cory Taylor. In the cover letter for their tax appeal that year, Taylor wrote that as her treatment options ran out she knew 'that no-one was talking to me about the most important thing, and that was that I was probably dying'.

My support for Karuna was sown decades before. I had wanted a Karuna for my mother and our family when she had cancer, to talk about what was unspeakable between us. Taylor had found this place and she wrote about that, saying that if she didn't have a terminal illness she'd be making the kinds of plans we do, looking ahead to travelling or to new projects.

I paused as I read Taylor's words, because I've never been in the situation of having what she called 'a mortal illness'. Nothing in my experience has called on me to look at my life that squarely and adjust to the knowledge that the end of my life is in sight. Taylor's way of putting it was that 'it means choosing whether or not to accept dying as a fact of life', and recalibrating.

Later, when I read her book, *Dying: a memoir*, I saw that she'd been able to write it because there wasn't any pretence. She knew that her life was ending, and Karuna had enabled her to write her book without worry, dread or despair.

DISCUSSING DEATH AND DYING

Quite frequently at a Death Cafe, someone will raise the question of what to say when a friend is going through this process of recalibration.

> In a group of strangers gathered around at a winter solstice Death Cafe, a young woman speaks of the difficulty she has expressing herself to a friend. The subject weighs heavily on her and has impaired the flow of friendship. A son describes trying to talk to parents who don't want to discuss their frailty, and how his attempts fail again and again. 'I just hit a brick wall every time. You have no idea how frustrating it is!' But another woman smiles, ready to find common ground with him.

We're not very experienced in this territory. We get together to be there. How do we sit with our discomfort when we don't have the right words for someone who has experienced bereavement? People at the Death Cafe share personal experiences and suggestions. The young woman knows she's not the only one who has felt concerned that their words might hurt, and I can see she feels better. I notice her realising that a simple acknowledgment would work well.

I often think of a reminder from a hospice outreach worker: 'Everyone is 100% alive until they're dead'.

Death: a love project

What a great concept. We can be frank in acknowledging the reality of illness and a person's concerns as they approach the end of life. At the same time there is life going on. 'Today I went to Bunnings – I'm going to make a wonderful change to the garden.' 'The Hawks aren't going anywhere this season …'

Many end-of-life practitioners talk about the difference between those who are able to embrace death and those who refuse it. Cory Taylor's book is a quiet exploration of how someone comes to see death as a matter of fact, and begins an easy conversation with the reader about the many dimensions of life that infuse dying. As a reader, I got the feeling that she would be able to manage letting go with grace. I hope that was the way it worked out.

Each person's circumstances are different. The person sitting with the prognosis, especially if the time frame is short, may be preoccupied with sifting questions of identity and the future. They may not want to talk to people outside their immediate circle, as much as their friends would like to see them. This can be hard to accept. Getting together with other friends who are similarly affected and talking it through can help. This could also be a good time to spend a reflective hour writing a letter, as Bobbi did for Glenda, or drawing a picture and putting it in the mail.

Death as a matter of fact

When faced with mortal illness, the support of social networks is as vital as the support of clinical specialists and support services. This is especially the case when a person decides to die at home or wants their friends and family to hold a vigil. Having this in mind will help with plans and conversations with service providers. Without feeling it is disrespectful or that you are pre-empting someone's death, it is useful to have a think about the arrangements that will bring people together to grieve, remember and celebrate afterwards.

Making your wishes clear

Taking the time to prepare a will and write down your wishes, regardless of your state of health or your age, will make a huge difference to those who survive you.

When my father died, my siblings and I searched cupboards and files looking for his will and wishes. We were in our early twenties. He had been sick all his life and we simply could not believe he hadn't left anything in place. We rang his doctor, his accountant and his lawyer. Had he mentioned anything to them? Finally we had to give up and begin the difficult process of acting without any instructions. Wrapping up his life in these circumstances did little to help us to grieve together or grow closer at a very difficult time.

Estate planning is just one aspect of planning for end of life. Another is an advance care directive. There is soaring interest in these, according to Advance Care Planning Australia.

You may already have financial and medical decisions in place but there's another element to planning ahead that I call 'wishes'. These are the things you would like others to carry out on your behalf, perhaps concerning the style of an end-of-life ritual, the choice of burial or cremation or the service providers you'd like. Putting your preferences down on paper can be helpful and save others having to come to an agreement at a difficult time.

If you have your will filed at your lawyer's office, remember to keep these wishes separate, ideally in an accessible place at home. They will be needed before your will is opened.

> At a grief and bereavement conference, a speaker who was in her early thirties made a strong impression on me. In preparation for their marriage, the priest had insisted that she and her husband make wills and define their end-of-life wishes. A few years later, while they were having a wonderful holiday in Europe, her husband died. In the midst of the suddenness, disarray and grief she held a kind of touchstone. His parents thought they knew what he would like. It was burial. She knew what he wanted and it

was not burial. Together they could act on what he'd committed to paper.

When I tell this story, young men and women who've moved to Australia and left their family and friends behind understand immediately. 'Yes,' one young man said. 'I need to explicitly connect my life here and my life there by making my wishes clear across continents.'

SUPPORTING EACH OTHER

It's easier to set aside time for a difficult or unappealing task when it can be done together. This is a natural thing for couples to do. But here's another approach. A group of friends get together four times a year to undertake 'heinous tasks'. These may be thing that they have put off, like writing a letter to an MP, mending clothing or, in my friend's case, finalising her end-of-life wishes.

When Glenda had cancer but was still doing pretty well, she asked a friend, Sophie, if she would come along with her to an event I was running in the city. 'Sure,' Sophie responded, knowing that Glenda always had her finger on the pulse of great cultural and community events. On the tram into the city, Glenda pulled out a light purple shawl adorned with tombstones from her bag, and told Sophie they were going to find out more about her funeral options. She wanted to have a trusted companion beside her as she became more familiar with what was out there.

CARRYING OUT WISHES

Once in a while I'll hear an old person say, 'Oh well, who knows if they'll carry out my wishes?' This saddens those who have no influence on the situation, like aged care staff and managers. It's normal to have preferences, but is also important to respect a person's wishes. Why is it that this often doesn't happen?

Some people are too self-interested to follow through on someone else's wishes. Others decide that they know better than what's written on paper. 'No, we won't donate his body to science, it doesn't feel right.' 'We won't have the coffin at the ceremony – the body in there isn't Dad anymore.' 'I know she said that about religion … but it won't feel right if we don't have prayers.'

When we write down our wishes, it's easy to assume that it is obvious why we are making these requests and how our lifelong values have influenced what we want. But if someone doesn't understand why a wish has been made, it's likely to be harder for him or her to carry it out.

Interesting surprises relating to people's wishes popped up at the workshops I ran at Melbourne's Sustainable

Death: a love project

Living Festival about planning sustainable funerals and vigils. I was discussing environmental values, but I was just as interested in the social dimension of rituals like vigils and the conversations we have in our families.

The attendees at these workshops were not people for whom rose gardens and green, well-mowed lawns conjured up eternal peace. They were looking for facts about how they could have the least possible impact on the environment when they died. On one occasion, a funeral director came along. She had visited suppliers in China and described in detail the terrible conditions in the factories that produce cheap cardboard, craftwood and chipboard coffins. We all shuddered.

Later, we formed into small groups to explore specific attributes of coffins and shrouds. Geoff had come in holding the view that he wanted his coffin to be sustainable and unpretentious. After talking with the rest of the group, he began to see this idea from his children's point of view. He'd never discussed with them this wish that he'd put in writing. Might they see a simple pine coffin as unattractive and cheap? Would they feel it didn't do justice to him or his family? Would such a box even appear shameful to them? He needed to talk to them.

Another group realised that a written wish to be buried in a shroud could be confronting, uncomfortable and difficult. How could they deal with this? Firstly, they could reassure their family members that shrouded burial is legal. Then they could sit down and look at pictures of different shrouds. If there were still objections, they might have to re-evaluate. Putting this choice in place would be a process rather than a directive. After all, they wouldn't be the ones carrying out their own wishes.

BODY AND ORGAN DONATIONS

Donating your body to science or donating organs or tissue can raise strong opinions and concerns. The idea that 'I am not my body' is a perspective that may have grown on the prospective donor through the process of ageing or after spending some time reflecting on life and death and what happens afterwards. The intention to benefit others is a generous motivation, and instructions are likely to be put on paper in this spirit. However, it's natural for children to be very attached to a parent's body. They may dread the thought of what happens to it after death. The idea of the body being stored or cut up may be horrific to them. If someone is going cold at this thought, they are not likely to be at ease with the donor's wish. Their reactions will also be difficult for those who want to do what has been directed. Acting on something so unfamiliar or unknown can be very frightening and raise an instinctive resistance.

Death: a love project

> The University of Melbourne's Body Donor Program coordinates donations to medical faculties across Victoria. It recognises that donation is valuable to all of society through the great opportunity it gives medical professionals in training. Each year a commemorative thanksgiving event brings together families of donors and medical students in a carefully curated ceremony honouring the generosity of donors. Julie went after her father donated his body. She was deeply touched to find herself in the midst of an event filled with life, warmth and gratitude. The professor who spoke made sure that everyone felt the appreciation of the whole medical field. The young medical student Julie talked to told her how he got utterly real about his future career after his first experience of anatomical dissection.

This may be exactly the love project you want. At the same time, there's a lot for family members to consider and talk about. It's worth taking time to do that together.

Making your wishes clear

It's best to express your wishes to those close to you ahead of time. When enough preliminary planning is in place, the remaining decisions can be put aside and reviewed at a time when there is more pressing reason to do so. When your wishes are considered and expressed in writing and conversation, the people who love you have something to act on together. The conversations you have with your family might also take into consideration the needs of children. You can find useful information on material choices and purchases in the final part of this book.

Consider your options

Before you decide to involve a funeral director, you might want to think about what you want and what your budget is. Given the size of the purchase, think of this as the equivalent of buying a new computer or getting a quote for a landscaping job. It's worth putting different options on the table, doing a bit of research and having conversations with friends. Consider what is important to you. At its best, an end-of-life ritual displays what the person who died cared about and helps people make sense of their loss.

'Ashes to ashes, dust to dust.' Even when hardly a breath of religious tradition remains, these words are a reminder that one day we too will be recycled and return to the

Consider your options

earth. It's human to want to ignore this, but this ensures that death remains the preserve of the funeral industry. For better or worse, death is their business. When a family arrives at a funeral home, it is the arranger's job to determine and meet their expectations, right there and then. This is very difficult when the people in front of them are often in shock and know very little about what lies ahead.

> Jill told me she enjoyed our meetings because I helped her to understand the funeral industry, which she thought of as 'the other side'. She came to me to prepare herself before she engaged with a funeral company or a cemetery. She wanted to lessen the burden on herself and her family later. She knew there was a lot she simply didn't understand but would need to make decisions about.
>
> An online comparison tool to 'find the best funeral' wasn't for her. Neither was searching through a myriad of products online. Price wasn't uppermost in her mind in working out an appreciative, community-focused way to honour her beloved husband, who would die in the coming months or years.
>
> Jill wanted to meet with me face-to-face. She was looking for dialogue. As someone with a large network of friends, she thought of the whole exercise as one where everything she learned and put in practice would be valuable to others at some time in the future.

Death: a love project

'Can you please tell me in detail what happens between the time when a person dies and whatever event we decide we're going to hold,' she began. I talked her through key times, places and actions. 'What's the difference between a coffin and a casket?' she asked.

'It's just to do with the shape of the box. A casket is rectangular, not shaped at the head and feet.'

Jill enjoyed learning about a system she knew little about and worked through the options ahead of time. She wanted to research where she might buy a burial plot. She wasn't comfortable with cremation. 'I've talked to a lot of friends, trying to understand their ease with it,' she said.

Jill dreamed of having the perfect event for her husband at the end of his life and shared her thinking with him as she went along. Over a few months, and three or four meetings, we worked it all out. She had started out with very little idea and finished up with a vision. She found a funeral director who offered a clear breakdown of their pricing structure so she could choose what she now knew she wanted and needed. We finished our work together. Sad as she was about her husband's illness and decline, it made her happy to know that 'all that' was taken care of.

Six months after her husband died, we met and she told me how the arrangements had worked out. She'd followed all the steps we'd discussed, including holding two events. I'd encouraged her, as a carer of some years, to consider how she could best take care of her own energy reserves.

> She'd decided not to do anything big too soon, but just bring family and one or two friends together for the first ceremony. A few weeks after that, they held a large celebratory community event.

Devoting time to considering these things early paves the way for smoother and more satisfying experiences. We can think and plan with greater clarity when we are well, competent and lighter-hearted. And although the topic might seem morbid, Jill actually found her investigations intriguing.

WHO IS A FUNERAL FOR?

When exploring death, dying and end-of-life rituals people often ask, 'Who is it for? Is it for the person who has died or those left behind?' And then there's, 'Well I'll be gone anyway, so who cares?' But we do care. Participants in my workshops remember the deaths of friends and family members, the circumstances at the time and their experience of the rituals.

They speak of values. Beauty. Practicality. Creativity. Faith. Elegance. Learning. Love. Generosity. A common conclusion is that when a ceremony is in tune with the values of the person who's died, the mysterious purpose of the ritual is achieved and people are happy. Jill's

Death: a love project

husband's 'big event' was held at a sporting venue. Glenda's bright coffin, with its orange, turquoise and red on rough timber and mermaid impressions, brought joy. A procession of cars following the hearse to the cemetery can work if there's a strong cohort of support. An event in a local hall for a community-minded person can be simple and memorable.

If you're planning a ceremony as a family, don't forget the person's friends and community. It would be sad to relegate them to simply being spectators, when they may have been long-term associates and will have stories and feelings they would like to share.

> If they are wishing to unburden others or thinking it's all too expensive, some people say 'I don't want a funeral'. Everyone has their own reasons for coming to an event that celebrates a life, but we all appreciate it when a ceremony tells a bigger story of the person than any one guest can know. We feel satisfied when we hear stories of different eras, accounts of special interests and adventures, how the person we knew dealt with difficulties and what made them happy. A memorable ritual is a marker for those left behind.

9

Dealing with uncertainty

More effective clinical treatments mean that the knowledge that a person is not well often gives way to the reality that they are dying over a long period of time. This is also true for illnesses like Alzheimer's disease. Part of the journey is experiencing grief and loss well before the actual death.

Life doesn't always go to plan. I witnessed this in Ballina, a coastal haven for retirees, south of Byron Bay in New South Wales. At the pedestrian crossing, many of the shoppers were quite slow and held up the traffic. Sadly, some of those who had moved here to enjoy their retirement did not age gradually, but were diagnosed with Alzheimer's disease. As writer-in-residence with

Death: a love project

Ballina Dementia Care, I got some idea of what they and their partners went through and how their carers rose to the occasion.

Above all, the carers talked about the uncertainty of not knowing what to do, what was coming next or how to go on. Each week they gathered – twenty people sitting in a circle, one by one describing day-to-day losses, frustrations and loneliness. They brought up issues like conflict between family members, terrible times when their partner went wandering and got lost, and the realisation that the days of being part of a tennis or golf or bowling club were over. Hardest of all was when someone said, 'A place has come up'. Their partner would be going into care. Those in the circle grieved many times before their loved ones died.

Our writing activities became an important ritual for the carers. Here they could make light of frustrations. 'Holy Saffron!' one man began. His men's group applauded his story of finding lost underwear in the roasting dish. Stories poured out about the trials of getting their partners dressed and ready each morning.

The writers, who were housebound from week to week, composed stories about nature, writing about beaches and lakes and picnic spots they loved. They explored what nourished them. One woman wrote about how she stood in front of her eye-level front-loading washing machine and watched the clothes circling and cycling. It reminded her that life is dynamic and changing, even though she felt trapped in dullness and languor. It gave her new energy.

I asked them what carers do, thinking of them as saints. They explained to me how they did what they did.

> *Saints more or less go on and do what has to be done.*
> *They don't stop and think.*
> *I suppose they all have a soft spot.*
> *They do think.*
> *They try to achieve a degree of normality.*
> *They need to be able to dissemble, contrive.*
> *They do these things in hope.*
> *There is no choice, it's as plain as that.*
> *Saints do what comes naturally.*
> *They try to escape reality sometimes.*

Bonnie made a book, a poem to a page, each a lesson she'd learned caring for her husband. The only plan she felt she could count on was to begin each day on a positive and open-hearted note. She chose the title 'Prepare to share'. She and her fellow writers were empowered and took to speaking at forums and submitting material to health bulletins and carers' newsletters.

Death: a love project

SECRETS AND TABOOS

Fears and taboos made their lives very difficult. Old friends were sometimes so uncomfortable they stopped coming around. One woman described this as a sad paradox. Their house overlooked the water, and during his illness her husband's frequently repeated invitation to everyone he met was 'Do drop over, we live by the river'.

The title of the residency was 'You have to laugh. You also have to cry.' The service's focus was carers, and its visionary manager knew that one of the greatest difficulties was talking to friends, family and neighbours about what was happening. Alzheimer's and other forms of dementia are very poorly understood. At the final event, when the writing was exhibited and the stories shared, everyone applauded this initiative. Writing was a unique way of bringing a much-needed conversation into the public.

Among the writings were pieces that no-one would ever read. One was a tragedy in many acts. Another invoked unbearable pain and bitterness. Several were lines of remorse. Their tellers wanted to be free of them. I copied each story onto white rice paper, rolled it into a scroll and closed it with red sealing wax. On the outside was the phrase that had prefaced the account.

Dealing with uncertainty

I could never tell anyone this. This is my secret. I have never spoken of this before.

Every so often at a Death Cafe, someone will say something like, 'It sounds terrible to say this but I just wanted to know when he would die, it had just been so long.' A contribution may follow about how difficult it is to keep going as a carer. 'I also really struggled.' We might hear what people did that helped, like taking regular walks, going to the beach (or imagining going to the beach), getting in touch with a friend or having a massage.

I still remember the friends I made in Ballina and how Bonnie used to talk about taking a breath. She was remarkable and it was easy to accept her advice. 'When you stop and take a breath, it'll even things out for you my dear,' she'd say. 'It'll make you more receptive and at ease, at least that's what I always find.'

I was invited to a number of funerals in the course of the Ballina residency, and was the celebrant at one. Alf in the men's group had cared devotedly for his wife, Maisie, for some years. I was friends with their daughter Jill. We planned a funeral that would honour Maisie's memories of her beloved Scots grandma. There was a wonderful rendition of 'The Bonnie Banks o' Loch Lomond' with the lyrics 'You'll take the high road, and I'll take the low road, and I'll be in Scotland a'fore ye'. This song is deeply familiar and ordinary, but at the same time pungent with mystery. Which is the high road and which the low road? What is the nature of love? How do we find our way home if not for the companionship of others who are right there with us, even though their experience and choices may be radically different from ours?

THE IMPORTANCE OF CONNECTION

One snippet from the Ballina project has stayed with me. It was something a professional carer said about kinship.

We're all related somehow, otherwise it wouldn't touch your heart so much.

The word 'touch' is physical. We had come into contact with each other. Heartfeltness allowed us to be related. Reading out loud what they'd written, people sometimes cried. Later they'd be smiling at someone else's story.

We have to cry, and laugh as well.

Dealing with uncertainty

Within uncertainty, there is a great benefit from sharing with others and avoiding isolation. Everyone grieves at different times and has different activities that nourish them. People speak of 'doing what needs to be done'. One of these things might be settling on your plans for end-of-life rituals well before a funeral director becomes involved at the time of death.

10

Young people and death

Like adults, children and young people benefit from being part of things, especially when the situation is out of kilter, as it is when someone has died. Children and young people are loved members of a deceased person's circle and can play a role in preparing for a funeral ceremony.

When I was young, many bereaved children and teenagers were kept from engaging with the reality of the death and prevented from attending funerals, even of their parents. Many ended up believing that they were responsible, that something they did caused the death. This can have lifelong consequences.

I was twenty when my best friend died. Her parents

and mine decided that it would be too upsetting for me to be at the funeral and I wasn't given the option of attending. For years, I had dreams in which she hadn't really died, I just wasn't trying hard enough to reach her.

Some years ago I heard children reflect on death in conversation with ABC Radio's Natasha Mitchell at Melbourne's Wheeler Centre. The children came from different backgrounds and ranged in age from eight to eighteen. The first question they were invited to respond to was 'Why are adults so nervous to talk about death?' They made a few suggestions: because they're sad, they don't want that weighed-down-ness. It's a taboo, no-one wants to be the one who brings it up. They hurt so much. The end of a person is like the end of the movie – it can be heartbreaking.

I wasn't the only person whose jaw dropped listening to their compassion for their parents' generation. They were funny, too. One young person talked about how you might never get around to planning for your death because you want exactly the right song for a funeral, and you know that by the time you die you will have changed your mind. They all agreed that when you're dead, you're dead, and there's nothing you can do about it.

The young panellists had had a month or more of preparation for this event, in dialogue with adult mentors and each other. In reality, adults need to be prepared to take the lead in conversations about death and end-of-life rituals. It is far better to address the subject of death than ignore it – what children have to say is often wise.

MAKING SENSE OF DEATH

This letter appeared in a weekend supplement under the heading 'Discuss It'.

My nearly eight-year-old daughter has decided she wants to be cremated with Rupert the Teddy Bear ('I couldn't ever imagine being without him') and have her ashes scattered over 'the prettiest mountain you can find'. Not a sad conversation, not a child obsessed with death – just a statement of fact; an acknowledgment that it will happen (she plans to die of old age, in her sleep).

I wonder how this mother and daughter's conversation started, and where they are now. Having a chat every so often helps people of any age prepare for the idea that death will happen, and imagine choosing to make arrangements that are comforting for those left behind.

In Melbourne, six men and women in their thirties meet each year on the anniversary of their friend's death in their final year of high school. She died by suicide and her friends were shattered. At the funeral they made a pact to be there for each other and honour her life every year. Now, as adults with many commitments, they speak of this ritual as something they will do forever. They notice the changes in each other as they grow older. The woman who told me this story became a mental health worker, having clearly understood the link between mental health and suicide in her friend's short life.

I know others whose lives were shaken to the core, during or soon after school, by a friend's suicide. They have also worked through their loss with friends, slowly making sense of the event and their loss. When Rebecca looks back on her friend Claire's death, she admits she had feelings ranging from deep grief to anger and relief. The experience changed her. She remembers her mother allowing her privacy but letting her know that she was there and wanted to be kept in the loop. That was reassuring and still is. Her mother occasionally asks, 'Do you think about Claire much? What are your feelings and thoughts now that ten years have passed?'

Death: a love project

> Talking with young people about death can be speculative and thoughtful. Sometimes it is suddenly necessary to talk. Being honest, open and respectful encourages trust. With any death, we often can feel we could have done something better or differently. A young person especially need to understand that circumstances are very powerful. However much one might want them to be different, no one can alter them. But everyone can do their best within them, through talking, caring for and respecting each other.

Taking care of relationships

During illness and in death, communication between family members can take all sorts of turns. It's natural for the stress and strain to contribute to edgy relationships. Everyone is juggling practical demands, grief, family life and other commitments. Circumstances vary, but working together well at a time of loss does make a difference. It's a truism, but everyone is doing the best they can as they navigate this unfamiliar territory.

> My Uncle John and Auntie Julie were a walking love project. In their village outside Cape Town in a volatile South Africa, they attracted kindness. Men from Congo, Malawi and Zimbabwe called Julia 'Mama'. They were also resolutely independent atheists.

Death: a love project

When Uncle John died, my brother and I hurried back to Cape Town. John had been in failing health for quite a while and we had anticipated his death, but we were still shocked when it came. We hadn't been able to honour our parents in a way that felt fitting and we wanted to do our best for our uncle. We planned a ceremony at the aged care facility so that people who could no longer drive could still attend. But some people wanted a more formal ceremony as well.

The funeral company was highly recommended. We explained what we wanted, gave the celebrant John's details and wrote the eulogy. We succeeded in getting a plain pine box but we had an expensive package foisted on us because that was the way the company worked.

When the day for the service came, we trekked out across the Cape Flats to the crematorium. The service began with the celebrant adopting the traditional formal-compassionate-solemn look. He got off to a flying start by calling John 'Michael'. We winced and hung our heads. Ten minutes into the service, he affected a meaningful pose and began praying in a rich voice. We could not have made it clearer that we did not want any prayers. At that moment, a great south-east wind blew through the chapel, and the door banged like heavy gunfire. Kabooom!

Despite this experience, and the bill and the week packing up a house full of a lifetime's hoarding, my brother and I grew into a newfound solidarity. Yes, we snapped at each other. I tend to act swiftly and my brother goes about

> things more judiciously. We got intensely annoyed and impatient with each other, and then we'd apologise and get back on the job. I came to appreciate how good he was at dealing with institutions in a tactful and insightful way. He saw that I had staying power and kept things moving.

The circumstances in which people die are different for every family, and every family has unique relationships. Mutual support may come naturally. Glenda was originally from Perth and saw her family infrequently over the years. When she was dying, her sisters came. They learned more about her life. When the local council sent good wishes and a huge floral arrangement, they realised that Glenda's gardening activities had attracted public attention and respect and were far more than a hobby.

FRAILTIES OF RELATIONSHIP

Sometimes close relations who have not spent much time together over the years need time to get comfortable with each other. At first, they may feel uneasy. The roles each person would normally play as part of an easy, unspoken understanding don't work as well. An offhand comment may turn an amicable discussion into a heated argument.

Different family members journey with a person through their illness in different ways and come into the process at different times. It's easy for someone who comes in later, who lives far away, has unavoidable commitments or has even chosen to keep their distance, to feel marginalised or isolated.

Anyone who has been very active in caring will have times when they feel put out. It is very difficult to bring others up to speed on choices, decisions and plans. It is hard to communicate the demanding nature of caring work. Resentment may come up. This is human, but it is best not to dwell on it for too long.

We're all in this together. We're all fumbling our way along. Even when it is overwhelming, hold in mind how important it is to respect another person's unique relationship with the person who has died. Do the best you can to acknowledge the feelings others are expressing.

Not everyone rises to the occasion when someone is dying. But even when it appears that they are not doing what you think needs to be done, they are still playing a valuable role. Bear with it. Everyone's efforts, personalities and tendencies are likely to seem more strongly etched than usual. At times like these, take a breath. Take some time out.

Taking care of relationships

The title of this book suggests death is a work of love. It's wonderful to act in this spirit, but these aren't always the circumstances in which we find ourselves. When time is on our side, it's more likely there will be moments to take space and come to terms with the frailties of relationship and keep doing our best. Waves of feeling ebb and flow during times of suffering and hit people at different times. Rituals can be jointly prepared to express what everyone feels is fitting for the person who has died. This may involve working with a third-party companion to make it a little easier to have difficult discussions and make important decisions.

12

Coordination and planning

After you say goodbye at the bedside, end-of-life rituals follow. If you are fortunate, there will be time to organise these at a comfortable pace. Nonetheless, it's important to know what's involved. There is a lot of scheduling, there are a lot of places people need to be or get to, and there are many roles and activities to consider. Some significant tasks include making and answering phone calls, organising the ceremony or the wake, collecting photographs, liaising with the venue and working out the look and feel, and communicating with the guests. This chapter is presented as a list to make the different tasks clear.

Overall coordination: It can make a huge difference if one person can be responsible for coordinating others and overseeing what needs to be done, especially when lots of people are offering to help. This doesn't mean one person does all the work or is the boss! It's just fortunate if circumstances make this role possible.

Communication: It will seem as if the phone never stops ringing. Think of notifying people as a shared responsibility. A message book is very useful. Write a list of people to be notified and put them in categories. In other words, prioritise your calls. Prepare yourself for the questions you need to answer. People will ask for details about the death, if a funeral has been planned, where and when it will be held, where they can stay if they're coming from interstate, and if someone can pick them up from the airport.

Ceremony: The conclusion of a life turns our thoughts to the life as a whole and its chronology. There are many ways of shaping a satisfying event. Think of what mattered most to the person. Consider having objects that tell a story – favourite pieces of art, cherished pot plants, a motorbike, and so on. Plan for fifty minutes – don't go too much over one hour. Try for balance. Spread out the music rather than having a predictable order of speakers followed by music. Having a coffin at your ceremony speaks about death though it's less common nowadays at end-of-life ceremonies. Families have different reasons for making this choice.

Venue: If you choose to hold a funeral in your home or garden, as Glenda did, there will be plenty of work that goes into setting it all up. The same goes for using a community venue like a local hall. This may be really good. People are often looking for something to do in the time after a death and are happy to help. When preparing, think about what it is about this space that lends itself to the ritual you want, such as people coming into the centre and going away from it, farewells or children's input. Remember you will have to clean up afterwards.

Home: There will be more people coming and going than usual. Generally there will be a lot of food delivered by kind friends and no space in the fridge to store it all. There will be errands of all kinds to run. Older children can be fabulous at looking after the younger ones.

Offers of help: Accept these. You are putting on an event that is as big as a wedding without much preparation time. An offer to vacuum and tidy the house can make a huge difference. You could even ask for help with this.

Look after yourself: Don't forget to nurture a place within yourself so you can rest and protect the sensibility of this time. Take time each day for a walk around the block, a nap under the doona or a coffee in a cafe. In a very unsettled time, some silence and sitting still can go a long way to help you process this new reality.

On the day: Be there ahead of time. Know that shedding tears while speaking or delivering a eulogy is absolutely natural and helps others experience the reality of loss. If you feel shaky, have a close friend stand alongside you.

> After your planning, and drawing on all the goodwill and skills around you, the ceremony is likely to be remembered as a perfect fit for that person. This is a demanding and satisfying love project. You may have been involved in activities like laying out or a vigil ahead of a more public end-of-life ritual. You may have found the right coffin or shroud. You may have given special thought to involving children in the end-of-life rituals. Some of this may have been discussed before death or in the deceased's written wishes.

13

Meaningful rituals

Rituals are a way of marking change at an important time, in a way that is significant and real to those who participate. This provides mutual acknowledgment and shared knowledge of what is important. End-of-life rituals are as varied as the people who choose and craft them. Elements that have a strong influence include the way the program is timed, the presence or absence of coffin or body and the way seating is arranged.

Arrangements that bring people together at the end of life centre on rituals of different kinds. The simplest thing will be powerful if done well. Confidence and authority breed confidence and reassurance. Everyone breathes and settles down when people perform their

Meaningful rituals

roles in a ritual in a way that shows they know what they are doing. This confidence comes from good planning and preparation.

> February 2016: Inside the chapel are people dressed in black or grey. The young men are wearing the closest they can get to suits. They are acting their way into a solemn and formal occasion. There is silence as we enter and the organist begins playing. We look at the photo – it captures him perfectly. The order of service is formal. 'The Lord is my shepherd, I shall not want …' The murmur of voices in the pews hushes. The minister steps up to the lectern.

> August 2016: His Essendon scarf is draped on the coffin. Posies and bouquets from friends' gardens are piled around it, along with many notes. In their different ways, each note says, 'I have never before met such an unassuming extraordinarily accomplished man. I'll try to learn from you, I'd like to do better.' Everyone gets the chance to see him for the last time in his coffin at the back of the church.

> January 2017: We wash the body with a cloth and fragrant oil in a basin of water. The family comes and goes, tidying the room, occasionally coming to say hello. The sheet is folded in such a way that sprigs of flowers are part of the fabric. The clothes have been selected and are sitting on the chair. Attention and intimacy inform every move.

> April 2017: My friend and I walk up the street together. I hardly notice the black hearse and the funeral company logo as we approach. The uniformed, name-badged assistants stand ready to greet the guests. I'm invited to sign the guest book. At the front of the chapel there are large, formal, yellow and white flowers. The coffin is at the front, under another huge floral array.

WHEN RITUALS GO WRONG

Everyone feels uncomfortable at a ritual that doesn't work. A ceremony like my Uncle John's, where the celebrant got the name wrong, or an outdoor gathering where there isn't a microphone and no-one can hear, produce distress and unease.

In the great myths of Western culture, the goddesses did not favour mortals who rushed or didn't get the rites correct. There was a causal relationship between the correct placement of the vessel or pouring of the libation and outcomes in the world. When things went pear-shaped, punishment followed. Bad stuff happened.

We don't think about ritual that way anymore. Yet things do go badly wrong when ritual has not been considered. I hear about disasters like this. 'I wouldn't have known the ceremony was actually about him'. The tellers of these stories live with regret and a sense that the life of the person wasn't properly honoured. They grieve for a long time over that.

WHAT DOES A RITUAL MEAN TO YOU?

Rituals are not only ecclesiastical or radical-hippie-mystical-pagan (although they can be, of course). Even if the word 'ritual' conjures up thoughts as varied as citizenship ceremonies on the 26th January or tribal dances in the rainforests of Brazil, it is worth cultivating your own contemporary understanding of ritual.

A well-planned ritual turns what might otherwise go by in a blur into something memorable. There is an intention. A ritual has a shape – a beginning, middle and end. Some events are delightful but can't find a way to end, which can ruin them. A simple thing like an introduction focuses attention. A pause at a certain moment draws attention to what is taking place, like a coffin being driven away.

Depending on how a space is prepared, we participate and think in different ways. The space of arrival is important. It puts the spirit of the occasion right at the door. On one occasion, the children were in charge of making gifts for guests to take away. They had bound sprigs of rosemary with a tag and their circle of activity was near the main entrance. My thoughts went immediately to the relationships these children had with the woman who had died.

I was once taken around a well-known funeral company's storage area and saw the shelves where they could grab 'the right stuff' at short notice. There was a mass of bits and pieces – crosses, candlesticks and soft toys – as if we carry our beliefs and values at surface level to be grabbed off a shelf on the run. I prefer to think of an order and beauty that is based on considered intimacy with a life and its story. This can comfort people deeply.

Look around and assess what needs to be done to make things feel right. Seating influences involvement, so a first step might be to think about how the chairs work in the space. Should they be set out in rows or in the round? There may be a perfect spot for the largest chair. There will be a place that is most natural to put the flowers, different sized tables and stools. Step back to experience the effect the arrangements will have on guests and alter anything that is off balance. Attention to detail can create something unforgettable.

MARKING GRIEF AND LOSS

A group of friends, colleagues and family can do a lot by simply holding the grief and loss of those closest to the person. Today, the pendulum has swung from the dark foreboding funerals of the past to celebrations of life, and parties. Glenda wanted a birthday celebration – her birthday was soon after she died – and she wanted her coffin to be at the centre.

For key theorists in grief and loss, the ritual of the funeral is seen as the first task of grieving. It's quite natural after a death to think, 'I can't believe it's happened' or 'It can't be over'. A gathering of family and community spells out that it is real and that everyone is impacted by the loss in some way. By making their loss public and acknowledging its effect, those closest to the person who has died have permission to be sad and to mourn, as well as remember the wonderful times.

It's vital to celebrate their qualities, relationships and achievements. The trend towards holding a celebration of life has been driven in part by cost efficiency in the funeral industry itself. It is easier and less costly to leave the coffin out of it, to organise the ceremony around a tried and true template, and use a PowerPoint presentation to convey the person's story. There's less risk if they omit the solemn moment of pallbearers lifting the coffin and use a gurney instead.

When we're invited to participate in the solemnity of long-practised spiritual tradition, we are reminded that death is also our fate. For those who are faithful, repeating liturgy that has come down through countless generations is comforting and deeply important. The words 'forgive us our trespasses as we forgive those that trespass against us' are a fresh reminder that by admitting mistakes, forgiving and making amends we keep love projects alive.

SOUNDS, SEASONS, IMAGINATION

The sounds of a ritual draw people together. Voices joined in singing. The resounding call of a taiko drum. The sweet essence of a song. When a young person has died and we are dumbfounded, music can hold a ritual together.

When rituals invoke the elements of life and the power of seasonal forces, they nurture us. When young children light a candle, their innocence brushes off on their parents and older siblings. Everyone joins in kinship with a world that's alive and full of power, one that we become estranged from when, in Joni Mitchell's words, we 'put up a parking lot' over so much of the natural world.

Wonderful imaginative acts put a rich new stamp on celebrations and everyday life. Picture supporters helping a woman in the later stages of an illness, who has baked for family, events and fundraisers her whole life, to bake teacakes for a party. Picture a ceremony for a beloved grandmother, the children firing flaming arrows into the sea from bows they've been working on all week. Picture a widow throwing petals on her husband's coffin.

> With an end-of-life ritual planned to suit the person and situation, you can feel confident about involving others. The ceremony will be remembered as a good one. This is important in navigating grief and loss. Ritual creates a feeling of being organised, purposeful and creative. This feeling can begin in preparation, in planning either someone else's or your own arrangements. With ritual in mind, thinking about children and their needs comes a little easier. A ritual of laying out the body and holding a vigil takes planning, and allows everyone to gently face the reality of death.

14

Involving children

End-of-life rituals shine when all the important people have contributed and played a role. Dignity is implicit when relationships are honoured. This is also true of children and their special relationship to the deceased, playing their part in what funeral director Amy Cunningham calls 'a fitting tribute'. Like her, I find that children take pride in creating such tributes. As hosts or guests they find a place among others. No-one is alone or disconnected from what is going on.

As a parent, it's natural to feel nervous about making a mistake that might hurt your child. This often accounts for a reluctance to talk directly to young people and children about death. The hardest thing is to see your

Involving children

child suffering and not know what to do. One thing to remember is that even though you can't stop a child feeling sad, you can support them by listening as well as talking.

Phrases like 'passed away' or 'gone' are sometimes preferred when talking about death. However, they may be confusing for children. Try to use words that are as simple and clear as possible. Be sure they understand that death is inevitable – nothing they did caused it.

Just as adults unconsciously shrink from the idea of being close to death, almost as if they could 'catch it', this concern is real for many children. Reassure them that it is safe to be around a person who has died. Give the child the option to come in to the room or not.

Preparation and support is key. 'Yes of course you can kiss her. Her body is quite cold now – the life is gone. It's her and it's not her.'

The account of a vigil by Joanna Macy earlier in this book describes children at ease in the room where their grandpa is laid out. There is plenty of evidence from the American home funeral movement that when everyone is at home with a person lying in honour, it is natural for children too. They go in and out of the room, talk to the dead person and play in proximity to them. This shared experience and ritual is life-affirming. It is made possible by conversations between adults and children.

When thinking about taking a child to a funeral, you can help by providing them with a framework. For example, anticipate the space and how it's likely to be set up. Talk to them about:
- where family and other people who are most directly affected are likely to sit
- whether the coffin will be there or not
- how long the ceremony will go for
- what roles people that they know may play
- what tone and emotional environment they might encounter.

Creating a picture for a child sets them up for a better experience. Some of these pointers would also help an adult going to a funeral for the first time feel a little more ready.

INCLUDING CHILDREN IN RITUALS

There are many ways of involving children in end-of-life rituals, and their presence will make a difference. The more the family takes charge of arrangements, the more scope there is to give them a role. Here are a few examples of how they could participate.
- Decorate the coffin or shroud.
- Choose the music.

Involving children

- Fasten flower posies.
- Put notes or tags on plants or other gifts to take away from the ceremony.
- Put a special object or message in the coffin or shroud.
- Make symbolic decorations, like a blessing tree using a branch and leaf-shaped cards on which guests can write words of encouragement to the family.
- Light candles.
- Tell a story, play music or sing, with a parent or friend standing alongside for support.
- Play a part at the gathering afterwards.

> The choices each family makes about involving children will be different. Fundamental aspects of a parent's contribution to a child's wellbeing at a difficult time are talking in simple clear words, being there to listen and comfort, and talking to them about what to expect. It is helpful to have some ideas about how children or young people can participate in the ceremony. Make sure your child is supported and isn't dwelling on the situation while others are busy with care or preparations. Be there to answer questions and check in regularly on how they are coping.

15

Service providers

End-of-life service providers range from traditional funeral directors to practitioners who work alongside the person and family for a period of time. Different approaches suit different people, depending on their hopes, needs and previous experience.

TRADITIONAL FUNERAL PROVIDERS

Reaching for the phone and calling a funeral director straight away is an automatic reaction to a death, even though there is no rush and no-one is obliged by law to use a funeral director. In Australia, most bereaved people will turn to a funeral company to help. You may have done this and had a perfectly satisfactory experience. Funeral companies undertake a number of tasks, including transporting the body to the company's premises and storing it, holding a meeting about the arrangements and carrying out funeral arrangements, including the legal paperwork.

Funeral companies work on the assumption that whatever a person's circumstances, they are entitled to a funeral that respects and honours them. Their job is to fulfil the task at different levels of service, from the most expensive to the most affordable. Many Australians and New Zealanders will have dealt with InvoCare, the biggest funeral company chain. Its suite of offers includes brands like Simplicity, Guardian, White Lady, Value Cremations (online-only 'No Service Cremation') and Le Pine. There are also local funeral brands trading under family names that are Invocare subsidiaries. In Victoria, Tobin Brothers is another corporate funeral company with a large presence in Melbourne. However, the majority of funerals in Victoria are still done by smaller, local, family-owned companies.

The use of 'From $...' pricing is common in the funeral industry, and when making a purchase you are well advised to be wary. Minimum prices may not be accurate. Bare Cremation's specific remit is cremation-only, that is unattended cremation, the return of ashes and death certificate. In 2021, Bare paid a penalty to the Australian Competition and Consumer Commission (ACCC) for allegedly misleading customers with inaccurate 'From pricing' on their website. Other companies have also had to pay penalties.

Inevitably in the business model of any large funeral company, time is money and the price range brings this home. For example, an exploration of what mattered to the person who has died can't be given time when you don't have the money to pay for it. Yet, as we have seen, taking time for enquiry and dialogue makes for a uniquely meaningful ceremony and experience at end of life. You will get better service and price by shopping around, and asking friends and family for recommendations.

The ACCC requires funeral companies to provide accessible pricing information. If you can't find it on a funeral company's website, there's reason to be distrustful.

In 2018, funerals come in at a no-frills $4–6,000, an average of $10–12,000, and a high end of $15–20,000. You may be eligible for a Services Australia (Centrelink) lump sum bereavement payment based on relevant criteria. You're advised to make the claim as soon as possible.

In 2024 a cremation only, purchased directly from one Victorian cemetery trust, GMCT, costs a little over $1,000. Throw in an hour's chapel service in attractive venues and the cost rises to $1,230. However you'll also have to add on certification, transport and storage costs, if sourcing them from a funeral director. A range of Australian companies offer cremation only. Comparing quotes and pre-planning is well worthwhile.

Today, the status symbols of large bouquets, elegant coffins and impressive hearses no longer matter as much. Many people say they would prefer the money to go to an important cause or to the next generation.

Now that it's normal to reach the age of eighty or ninety, we may have less money to spend on a funeral. It may come as a relief to explore practical, financially manageable alternatives to conventional commercial funerals. A number of things make this possible. Firstly, speaking out when meeting the funeral director or arranger. Secondly, coming to an agreement on selected services. For example, 'We'll need transport, but we won't need staff in attendance during the ceremony'. Thirdly, avoiding expensive products or venues.

The funeral industry business model assumes that consumers will also buy products such as burials, cremations and urns. Then there are the 'extras'. This is where people incur expenses they may not have expected for things they don't want, like catering, personal online tribute websites and memorials, flowers and having thank you cards sent on their behalf.

You may be asked questions like, 'We can organise the flowers – would you like us to do that?' or 'You might want a personal tribute website … they're a lovely way of inviting friends and families to make tributes … would you like that?'

You are in charge. If you need time to think or discuss things further with others, ask for time before making a decision. Above all, you want the arrangements to feel fitting.

In Victoria, South Australia and Western Australia, where cemeteries and crematoriums are managed by statutory trusts, you can buy burials and cremations directly from the trust. These trusts are exempt from GST, so the savings can be substantial. On an $8–10,000 grave, a saving of $800–1,000 can make a big difference. You can find price lists on the cemetery and crematorium websites.

In New South Wales and Queensland, InvoCare owns many cemeteries and crematoriums as well as funeral companies. Their absorption of all aspects of the funeral domain into a single business doesn't help consumers who wish to economise in this way.

Some funeral companies declare themselves to be independent alternatives and offer a more intimate and environmentally friendly service. Some make strong claims to be 'green'. You might want to ask around about others' experiences or enquire directly, ask questions and put your preferred choices to them.

A funeral is a large purchase and it makes sense to have a list of things that you must have, things you would like and things you definitely don't want. The list will be different for every person or family. For those undertaking a family-guided funeral, although you are not required by law to use a funeral director, you are required to comply with relevant state legislation. A small, flexible funeral company can help with this if requested.

HELPFUL QUALITIES IN A FUNERAL DIRECTOR OR ARRANGER

You should be able to arrive for your initial appointment with a list of what you want and they should not be surprised or disconcerted by that. They should welcome questions and support you in your decision-making.

They should be accustomed to the slower pace of a bereaved person's thinking and respect that. The company's literature would identify the service and product components of the purchase. Transport, laying out, storage and ceremonies are services. Urns, flowers and coffins are products.

They should listen and take directions. This should include checking and repeating back names to be sure they've got them right and can pronounce them correctly.

You could ask them about their protocols for removing the body from the house or hospital room. This is a time of great transition. Your question might come as a surprise to them, but will give you an indication of whether they consider this ritual important.

A SUPPORTIVE JOURNEY

Far fewer people today are members of faith communities. For those who are, there's often a stated interest in each other's wellbeing. In a sense community and spiritual support at the end of life is part of the package. When my elderly neighbour was very ill, members of her congregation came round and they took a lot of care of her. Her pastor was available.

Doulas and end of life companions fill this gap for lay people and service providers other than funeral directors are increasingly sought after. You might use a death doula, an end-of-life practitioner or a home funeral guide. As a client, you would usually make first contact before you die or before the person you are caring for dies. After that, you would engage in an ongoing companionship over a period of time. This may span the last stages of illness, death and the funeral, celebration of life or memorial. You can expect practitioners to be well set up, for example, with access to an independent funeral director and cooling equipment for vigils.

The psychosocial, practical and spiritual dimensions will all have a place. For example the term 'doula', the traditional name for someone who assists a woman during labour, has become an equivalent term for someone who accompanies another person on the journey of dying. Unsurprisingly, many death doulas are former nurses who are familiar with palliative processes and laying out a body.

End of life practitioners often bring an intention to work in an intimate and engaged way with a family. Their clients want something other than a standard end-of-life product or experience. Practitioners also bring skills from previous work. For example, Victoria Spence, a well-regarded Sydney arts professional, brings her experience with ritual and a rich critical perspective. I have long experience as a facilitator and educator and with ritual and writing.

Even if you are intrepid and resourceful, there's good reason to be cautious about going it alone. Someone who knows the territory can be helpful as you work things out.

When the end of life comes after a long journey with palliative care, everyone is tired. Even if there's a clear plan in place, a third-party organiser can bring new energy and consistently hold the vision in mind. With my friend Glenda, I took up the role of companion, or in her words 'buddy', and was available to her and her partner. They wanted a one-stop shop for their information and service requirements. By choosing this approach, the care of her body and end-of-life celebration were tailored to their needs and everyone else could conserve their energy at a very difficult time.

In one family, the mother died very suddenly. One son flew in from overseas. Other close family members travelled from interstate. Travel is tiring. They needed to adjust to being back home in the face of a huge loss. They had plenty of ideas about what they wanted. 'We need a bit of help,' they said when they brought me in to the planning. 'We need space to grieve.'

For those who are part of a faith tradition creating the ritual involves leaders, congregation, friends and sometimes musicians or choirs. Holding a ceremony in a familiar place of worship is a great help to the bereaved. For others, as expectations change, we see people bringing end-of-life rituals home and holding them in lounge rooms, gardens, galleries and community halls. Some people approaching death want to take charge of where and how things will happen after they die, with well-planned vigils at home.

Going outside established social expectations might feel unsettling. But if you lean towards trying a different approach or doing things very simply, there are plenty of people who have successfully kept the body at home, chosen a low-cost or homemade coffin, painted

Service providers

it and transported the body to the cemetery themselves. They've picked their own flowers. They've engaged their own caterers. They've brought a plate.

> End-of-life service providers can play different roles. You can explore a range of options and their pricing. You might want to take into account the particular circumstances of your family, friendship network or community. You might consider service providers in light of their capacity for coordination and planning for this time. You might want to have a discussion about what's involved in a ritual of laying out and vigil. You may just want to have conversations about your plans, or you may be ready to make important decisions.

16

Vigils and laying out

Vigils are as much about the deep pause in ordinary routines and nurturing family and community relationship as about care and attention to the body. Some things that motivate people to choose this approach include giving everyone time to deal with dying and bereavement, honouring someone important, undoing a fear of death, creating beauty in transition, having the support and presence of friends in an everyday environment, singing and making things more natural for children.

> 'He looked calm, handsome and noble … the next two days people came to pay their respects, a steady flow of friends and neighbours, some returning more than once,' wrote Joanna, remembering her husband's laying out and vigil.

Vigils and laying out

The funeral industry's process of transferring the body to their premises from the deathbed at home or in hospital is almost too efficient. It is common for the body to be gone within an hour. This is especially sad for anyone who has been a carer in a home palliative situation. I know of one person who, seven years later, is still mourning how abruptly her father was taken away after they had been in ongoing intimacy for months.

A vigil allows the shock of a sudden death to subside sufficiently to allow loved ones to adjust to the reality of their world having changed completely, and be actively part of a calming ritual with its own routine. Recently a grandmother said to me of her daughter, who had lost her son, 'She birthed him. She has to go through that process of seeing him out of life now.'

GLENDA'S VIGIL

Glenda died in the early hours of the morning, after a long illness. It was strange how quiet it was when we turned off the oxygen. The low-pitched sound and regular pops had been in the background for weeks. We stayed by her until dawn. When my colleague Pippa arrived, we moved Glenda to the front room.

We took up the slow process of washing and dressing her, during the comings and goings of family, and made the final arrangement of candles and flowers. She was beloved in her community and her friends were broken-hearted when she died. In the early afternoon, people arrived to visit and spend time saying goodbye. Some simply laid flowers or spoke their wishes. Many sang farewell songs. They left satisfied and surprised. They said how being present with the reality of death in a beautiful, calm space had helped them to accept what only hours before they'd found unbearable, unthinkable. It helped them come to terms with the fact that she would not be around anymore.

At Glenda's vigil, she was as elegant, beautiful and dignified as she was in life. I remember the flutter of surprise when she announced that she would wear the sequined turquoise evening dress. Even she was a little surprised. It was a great choice.

DYING IN HOSPITAL

In hospitals, nurses no longer do the work of laying out. This is now the job of the funeral company. Not many families get time to sit quietly with the person who has died, even if they were there during the death. They don't think to ask for this or for assistance to wash the body themselves. And it may not be something staff on the ward expect either.

When one family's father was dying, I suggested that they begin preparing the nursing staff for the idea that the family would like to stay on at his bedside for a while after he died. They found the staff kind and helpful, even though the request was a bit unusual. Their ritual was to get take-away coffees and pastries and sit around the bed for a few hours, talking and remembering. At first, one sibling was reluctant to bring her son, but when she found out that his cousins were coming she changed her mind. It was very simple. And very helpful.

Sometimes the person wanted to die at home, but things didn't turn out that way. In this case, it is still possible to bring them home with the help of the funeral director. Most hospitals will not allow anyone but a registered funeral director with transfer equipment and vehicles to undertake this task, based on their occupational health and safety and public liability requirements.

DYING IN RESIDENTIAL AGED CARE

In some residential aged care facilities, particularly religious-based nursing homes, care staff or nurses wash and lay out residents who have died so that the family can spend time with them. The ritual of washing the dead body could be seen as a last, simple act of love, one that family members might share if they like, or they can come later when the body is ready. When someone dies at a great age, washing the body and laying it out can be a real laying to rest. If you'd like to be involved at that stage, make sure that the care staff and nurses know. Again, if you'd like to bring the deceased person home for a vigil, you can do that with support from a funeral director.

KEEPING THE BODY COOL

People often ask if having a body at home is safe. It is, provided that effective cooling is in place. There are various unobtrusive and easy cooling methods from flexible esky sheets or 'blankets' and slim ice bricks, to cooling plates, which many independent practitioners loan out. In winter, or for a short vigil ice sheets are fine. Even in summer with air conditioning set very cool, they will suffice. In warmer weather and for a longer vigil, a portable cooling plate cools the body and is amazingly quiet and efficient. It's helpful to have the assistance of someone with experience.

Vigils and laying out

REGARD FOR THE BODY

It is hard to imagine something you've never seen. It takes preparation to have the confidence to do something you've never done before. Putting a plan in place can be thoughtful and light-hearted. What would I like to wear when I am dead and laid out? It's quite a question.

Those from cultures and spiritual traditions where rituals have the dead person's body at the centre are more at ease. I recommend the Japanese film *Departures* for its demonstration of companionship, witnessing, earthy humour, dignified body preparation ritual, beautiful costuming and regard for the body.

When I discuss vigils, Theonie, a second-generation Greek colleague, gives me a look that says, 'What else would you do?' Eamm, a friend from my tai chi group, remembers the kids in his neighbourhood in Malaysia heading off as a gang to see the old folks who had died down the street. They laugh at our nervous Aussie reactions.

It may seem odd to suggest that anticipating a slow after-death process might offer comfort to a dying person. Attendance by the beloved, through the dying process into whatever the next phase might be, is what Pablo Neruda requests of his lover in these lines:

Death: a love project

When I die, I want your hands on my eyes:
I want the light and the wheat of your beloved hands to
pass their freshness over me once more:
I want to feel the softness that changed my
destiny ...

> Vigils are comforting and make death imaginable. In the time after a person has taken their last breath, there is a calming effect in slowing down and staying close. If this approach appeals to you, make it part of your explorations. Talk about it with your children if you imagine your grandchildren might be involved, and make sure your wishes are clear. You might have a particular kind of coffin or shroud in mind, or be interested in different options for interring your body or ashes.

17

Burials and cremations

Attitudes to cremation and burial can come with deep-seated feelings, or simply be chosen because it's been done in the family before.

At my stand at Dying to Know Day in Melbourne's Federation Square, I talked to passers-by about death all day. A do-it-yourself shroud sparked many conversations, as did a colourful handmade coffin and a few poetry books.

One woman sat for a while, sewing hearts on the shroud, and then came over to talk about the coffin. 'It'd be a pity to burn something so beautifully made,' she said. I agreed, but for some people it was worth it for the qualities it introduced when people gathered around it, bringing flowers or tributes.

'How do you plan to go?' I asked.

She said she was trying to make up her mind. I quickly realised that for her the idea of putting a body in a cremator was visceral and painful.

'I don't know,' she said, laughing and a little embarrassed. 'It's something to do with the everlasting fires of hell!'

I reassured her that she's not the only person who can't stand the thought of cremation. For others, the idea of being buried and left underground is just as horrible.

She was brought up Catholic. We talked about the time when cremation was basically forbidden for practising Catholics. She admitted that she'd have to take more time exploring her deep-seated beliefs and feelings if she was ever to write instructions saying, 'Cremate me'. The church's ruling was changed back in 1963, but the legacy of the past lives on.

PLANNING AHEAD

People who are pragmatic and organised can feel quite pleased with their end-of-life plans. This is the case for Gerard Windsor. He was in the habit of scanning the funeral notices in the *Sydney Morning Herald* and picked up the information that descendants could apply to renew rights to hold prime real estate gravesites.

In an essay, he anticipates being laid to rest in Sydney's ocean-facing Waverley Cemetery.

> *The view you get from Waverley is so sunny and majestic and fresh-aired and teeming with melodious ghosts that you can't help thinking 'It is good to be here now' – and that delight spontaneously overflows into, 'It will be good to be here in future …'*

Generally, burial comes with two purchases. The first is the site. The second is the burial itself, as a charge is incurred for digging the grave, having staff on site and filling in the grave. It can be very satisfying to have spades and go to work shovelling after a burial, but cemetery managers find that few parties have the combined strength and resolve to complete the task. If you want to fill the grave in yourselves, be very clear that you are organised and responsible. Also be prepared that you might be charged for the service as a matter of course.

DIFFERENT VIEWS

Following family tradition, as most people do, I'd always thought of myself as a cremation person. For a start, it's much cheaper than burial. I had the opportunity to visit many cemeteries through my role on the community advisory committee of Melbourne's Greater Metropolitan Cemeteries Trust. Some cemeteries, like the one in Coburg, are old and have run out of space. Others like Templestowe are old and have found some more room, and yet others like Fawkner and Altona are still in the prime of their working life. There are also greenfield sites out in the growth areas.

I came to see that, with enough investigation, I'd probably find a spot where I wouldn't mind being laid to rest underground. My siblings and I had never been able to visit our parents after their death. In future, when a child among my descendants is puzzled about death, their parents might take them to the cemetery to visit my grave and put flowers on it.

At the Greater Metropolitan Cemeteries Trust, I learned that management in perpetuity is the core precept that informs cemetery management practice in Victoria. When ashes are interred or a body is buried in a cemetery, they ensure that they will not be neglected in coming decades. Cemeteries offer stability and continuity, whether in graves, crypts, memorial walls or under brass plaques around a tree. If an outdoor niche wall for cremated remains is cracking, the cemetery cares and does something about it.

Management-in-perpetuity is factored into the pricing of cemetery services. This accounts for grave fees skyrocketing in Victoria, which has in-perpetuity burials.

Each burial gives the managing trust a long-term obligation, which could also be seen as a debt, to maintain the grave in the cemetery context.

We visited the cremators and chapels at major cemeteries. Cremation is much more popular, and less profitable, than burial. Since cremations produce a fairly small profit, there's an animated interest in the sale of memorials, niches for ashes and ornaments that hold ashes. At our meetings we were often asked our opinion of some lovely new item. There was never quite enough time on the agenda to say!

Glenda didn't have any interest in being buried. Her family was in Western Australia and she wanted her ashes divided so that some could be returned there. She didn't want her ashes hanging around, so she didn't want a fancy container. She wanted to be cremated with the least impact.

> Burial and cremation are personal choices that are often preformed in people's minds but can invite discussion and deliberation about their merits. Cemeteries are places that we often speed past in the car, not seeing much more than the grey of marble and granite or the walls and fences. Cremators are many and various and it is a good idea to investigate what distinguishes them from each other.

18

Coffins and shrouds

There is a vast range of choices when it comes to coffins, including cardboard coffins. Shrouds are becoming a more familiar choice, and there are numerous kinds and ways of obtaining them. If you choose a shroud, you will need a transport coffin, which are available from some funeral companies.

I've heard a few people say that when they were taken into the showroom of coffins, they were dumbstruck. On wall-mounted shelves under bad lighting, sat grandiose gold-plated coffins, old-fashioned looking coffins made of stained chipboard and cardboard, and even contemporary woollen caskets. They were sure they knew what they wanted beforehand, but faced with such a huge range, how could they even think, let alone choose? One woman said that it wasn't that she was pressured, it was just all so confronting that she made a quick choice that she knew even at the time she'd be unhappy with forever.

CARDBOARD COFFINS

Not all cardboard coffins look like cardboard. A cardboard coffin can be the spitting image of a regular top-end coffin, moulded, stained and veneered to achieve a luxury effect. Needless to say, not every cardboard coffin is cheap. Any cardboard coffin must have specifications that show it will stay firm while carrying significant weight.

An inexpensive green or eco-funeral will probably include a cardboard coffin. At the lower end of the range, they are produced in China. In 2017, the Chinese government moved to fix the problem of factories ignoring emissions standards by penalising offending owners. Higher standards of coffin production can only be good for Chinese air and rivers. In Australia, burning coffins made with better quality glues and veneers will help reduce pollution. If you're planning on using a cardboard coffin, it's good to ask for evidence that it has been manufactured sustainably. Reputable companies will be able to produce this.

Death: a love project

SHROUDS

Harriet, one of my oldest friends, consults me about her funeral options. She wants the least waste of materials and can't see the point of an expensive coffin going up in smoke or being buried six feet underground. If she were to go in a coffin, she'd like one made from recycled timber. One of her nephews or grandkids could make it. But lately she's been thinking about a shroud.

I tell her that a shrouded body still needs to be delivered to the cemetery in a closed coffin. Some funeral companies and end-of-life practitioners will have a transport coffin that can be used for the funeral and the journey to the cemetery. The charge is basically for rental. If you want to avoid waste, it makes even more sense than a plain pine or cardboard coffin.

Harriet talked about shrouds with Maryam, her English language student, who turned out to be quite open to chatting about death. Maryam told her that when someone in the Muslim community dies, the family goes to the Imam who simply cuts a length of fabric off a roll of material for the shroud. This long and well-understood tradition has a no-frills way of fixing the shroud. From Maryam's description, Harriet learned that the process is simple and deeply comforting to the bereaved.

Harriet thinks she will consider this. Yet, like others who are choosing shrouds in our culture, she's a first-timer and the same goes for her family and friends. She says she'd like me to help. We could make one so that her daughters will see it lying around and get used to the idea. Or she could buy one – perhaps something elegant and beautifully sewn. Lovely qualities like colour and fabric texture would make sense, since the process of laying out a body and shrouding it is careful and sensual. There is wrapping, folding and tying of knots or bows. Most are made of silk, cotton, linen or hemp – all natural materials that will decompose.

Given that Harriet feels strongly about the environment, she might end up using a favourite old blanket for a shroud rather than silk that has been produced overseas at the expense of subsistence crops. She wouldn't be alone in wanting that simplicity, and that choice might work well, as long as her family feels comfortable with it.

Death: a love project

> The management of our end of life carries environmental, economic and social considerations. For some, a recycled or simple pine coffin could be seen as too cheap. If you're keen not to waste new materials and want to be cremated, it might make sense to use a certified cardboard coffin, which imitates more conventional veneer-finished products, or invest in a beautiful product made by a carpenter from recycled timber. For others, a blanket or a sheet might be perfectly fine.

19

Natural burials

How do you deal with, make sense of and remember the life and death of someone close to you if cremation and scattering of ashes doesn't appeal and there's nothing about the cemeteries you've seen that attracts you? Natural burial takes into account organic processes and can have wonderful aesthetic qualities as well.

There is a move towards a softer, more organic version of the traditional cemetery, described variously as green, eco or natural burial. The popular documentary *A Will for the Woods* describes how the dream of having a natural burial can provide great comfort to a person preparing to die. For those whose planning is informed by valuing a sustainable, low-impact lifestyle, natural burial may be attractive.

The brilliant 19th century Australian lyricist Henry Kendall wrote these lines to a young mother, perhaps his wife. The poem is titled '*On a baby buried by the Hawkesbury*'. The reader feels the comfort drawn from the river and nature.

> *The gold of the grass, and the green of the vine*
> *And the music of wind and water*
> *And the torrent of song and superlative shine*
> *Are close to our dear little daughter*
> *The months of the year are all gracious to her …*

People are increasingly searching for this kind of grace in their lives. Many people believe that natural burial is less environmentally harmful than cremation. Imagination also comes into play. There's a natural sensibility about returning to the earth and having a tree planted on top of you that your remains will nurture. Many who have attended the annual Sustainable Living Festival events I've run on funerals believe that death, like birth, is an organic, holistic and cyclical process. They say that is the way they want to go.

NATURAL SETTINGS

On an ABC 'Life Matters' forum, following a program with a natural burial expert from the UK, Shirley made a contribution that reflected many others' views:

'What a lovely thought – returning to the natural cycle of life. My family could visit me and have a lovely day out at the same time. Please make this happen. This is so natural. Also no eucalyptus (fire hazard) on top of me, and bird-friendly shrubs, please!'

Michael countered, 'I don't quite understand this misty, romantic view of natural burial, as if it's somehow beautiful to be buried in such a natural way, and returning to the elements, and all that ...'

The aesthetic of natural burial is compelling. Melbourne artist and clothing designer Pia Interlandi spent a rich period of her life helping with the early development of Clandon Wood, an award-winning natural burial preserve in the UK. Clandon Wood has the aesthetic qualities that many people look for in a burial site. The bare landscape has been transformed into a wetland, wildflower meadows, an orchard and a light-as-air pavilion. When Pia speaks, people's understandings of death and burial are transformed.

In purely practical terms, the key criterion for natural burial and an efficient composting process is burial at three feet. In recent years, six feet under has lost its place as an immovable standard. Natural burial advocates have challenged cemetery managers to accept shallower burials at Victoria cemeteries. In effect, a shallower grave means that there is no extra room to bury another member of the family in the same grave later on.

At the moment, the majority of Australian natural burial grounds are hybrids, set among regular cemeteries and memorial parks. Cemetery managers have often put brakes on the natural burial movement, insisting that there isn't sufficient customer demand. However, as natural burial expert Joe Sehee from the US Green Burial Council argues, it would be unusual for restaurant goers to request a dish that is not on the menu.

Cemetery managers also tend to say that their spaces have great natural settings already. They are satisfied that they can offer natural solutions like bio urns where you can grow an individual tree out of your loved ones cremated remains. Nowadays with climate change and increasingly harsh summer conditions, establishing trees is increasingly difficult. Most US and UK cemeteries don't have this challenge.

An early bushland cemetery went into operation in the early 2000s in Lismore, in the rainbow region of northern New South Wales. Customer demand was based on strong down-to-earth values. This style of cemetery made perfect sense. It enhanced the natural

Natural burials

environment, and the land use aligned with a koala habitat management plan for the surrounding area.

In Adelaide, around the same time, an independent MP drove a project to establish the first natural burial ground, Wirra Wonga, at Enfield cemetery. He imagined this form of land use enabling revegetation as well as providing peaceful endings. Wirra Wonga's popularity led to the development of a second natural burial site at Smithfield, which was laid out around a wildflower preserve.

Canberra set aside a portion of Gungahlin Cemetery for natural burial in 2015. The cemetery aims to locate graves so that they do not disturb existing trees or other vegetation, or cause erosion.

Pinaroo in Perth was developed as a natural bushland cemetery and planted with natives. Memorials are restrained. The landscaping features water and bushland paths.

Melbourne's Southern Metropolitan Cemetery Trust has achieved a long held goal of establishing a natural burial precinct at their Bunurong Cemetery. Here there is a boulder marking the arrival space of the area on which the names of those interred are recorded. Otherwise there is no grave marking, simply GPS location coordinates. For some people the absence of a marker, however small, can make this style of interment unacceptable.

Other options within easy reach of Melbourne are Healesville and Lilydale, which both have natural burial sections within traditional burial grounds. A little further afield in Queenscliff (Moonah Walk in Queenscliff Cemetery) and Traralgon (Gippsland Memorial Park) there's a commitment to indigenous plantings and natural values.

> Natural burial aims to enable a body's recycling and doesn't add anything harmful to the earth. At its best, it contributes to enhancing land, water and environment through the cemetery's design and management. The aesthetic values of natural burial, such as being in a peaceful place in the country or in a well-designed recess in a conventional cemetery, may be as important to you as its ecological integrity. You may also be thinking of those who will visit the site as part of the grieving process, or in years or decades to come.

20

Environmental impacts

Cremation can benefit the natural world. If you care about energy and land use, it can be a positive choice with different benefits to natural burial.

When Glenda asked me questions like, 'How do you see cremation? So much energy and such high emissions in climate change,' and 'Is natural burial environmentally positive?' I couldn't answer her in a black-and-white kind of way.

It would be tough for anyone to argue that a funeral, probably the most difficult event a family will ever plan, could or should be rigorously evaluated for how it might impact on the environment. However, this doesn't satisfy people who have lived with a small carbon footprint all their lives and don't want their death to add to the world's problems.

In Australia, natural burial hasn't yet found its footing exactly. A natural burial can somewhat reduce environmental impacts. However, few such burial grounds have been designed to make a meaningful difference to the environment. Some places do preserve existing pieces of bushland and hence are refuges for native plants and grasses, and a source of seed for future propogation. Planning for attributes such as a mix of plants native to the area with different lifecycles and habits, consideration of animal, bird and pollinator habitat, and plantings to achieve carbon reduction, deserves more emphasis. Qualities such as a peaceful aesthetic or being removed from the orderly headstones of the rest of the cemetery are natural in another way.

ENERGY AND CARBON

It is also relevant to know what goes on with cremators and how the funeral industry deals with carbon emissions and energy efficiency. The UK Natural Burial Centre suggests that the energy for an average cremation equals a month's domestic energy use by a single person. But there is no 'average' cremation – it's a matter of choosing a cremator that is new, state-of-the-art

Environmental impacts

and that minimises emissions. Older, inefficient cremators tend to remain in service for a long time, as they are well-engineered and get along fine with replacement spare parts. But they are more polluting.

Melbourne's Greater Metropolitan Cemeteries Trust's annual reports state that the organisation manages nine cremators and started metering energy use for the first time in 2012. Five years later the data were positive, that is, energy use falling slightly, despite a higher number of cremations.

The annual reports of the funeral giant InvoCare show that they have been aware of energy and carbon for some time. In 2007, as one of the 200 largest listed companies in Australia, they started taking energy and carbon into account in their business practices in response to a federal requirement to report greenhouse gases. In 2010, InvoCare took the step of voluntarily disclosing carbon emissions to a global standards body. In 2018, they no longer do this, possibly having decided their emissions position is adequate or improving.

Anyone can do a simple online transaction to take care of carbon emissions. Cremation comes at a fairly low cost. A cremation purchase can go hand in hand with a purchase of carbon offsets – $500–$1000 will easily offset a cremation and there are numerous reputable retail suppliers. Greenfleet has been offsetting through planting native forests for many years and has projects that are officially accredited through energy reduction and clean energy policy frameworks. A loved one's death and the choice of cremation can contribute to planting trees for the future and nurture a healthy mix of plants, animals and pollinators.

The significant development in organic, holistic body disposal now is the US-based Recompose. Founder Katrina Spade broke through funeral industry norms and pioneered the process of body composting at scale, with beauty. The start up attracted substantial investment for a completely new model of body disposal. In a relatively short time it has found legal acceptance in many states with others having introduced legislation to legalise human composting.

Australia has a small population, and as with technologies like Aquamation that are established elsewhere, we may not see composting introduced here for some time.

BENEFITS AND COSTS

If you are thinking about cremation, there is another meaningful dividend you might not be aware of. After burning, most cemeteries recover rare metals from fillings and implants. These metals are highly polluting if they are not taken care of. They are also a finite global re-

Environmental impacts

source and worth a fortune. Melbourne cemeteries have been capturing these precious metals for years and shipping them to Europe for recycling. The Greater Metropolitan Cemeteries Trust has directed the proceeds to the National Centre for Grief and Bereavement.

In the meantime, bear in mind all the trade-offs involved in any eco-friendly action. With cremation, think of land use. If there were no cremations, there would be infinitely more land taken up by cemeteries. In major cities, burial for all would simply not be sustainable. Cemeteries are now some of the largest tracts of public land in the city and are vital spaces for recreation – albeit in different forms than were dreamed of by 19th and 20th century town planners.

The scope of cemeteries of the future has been little explored and there are very few visionary models. In 2017, the Centre for Death and Society at the UK's University of Bath called on designers to imagine what the cemetery of the future might look like. Columbia University's winning entry, Sylvan Constellation, was dreamlike, beautiful and innovative – it's worth a google.

Death: a love project

> Over the years, we've grown used to organic certification on food products and considering environmental values in clothing, cars and lighting. It's relatively easy to find information in the print and electronic media to support our choices. However, services like cremation and burial, and the products associated with them like coffins and shrouds, also need to be scrutinised. Someone looking for five-star environmentally-friendly products may find it frustrating. It is better not to choose products in a rush.

21

Imaginative visions

At this time, in the world we live in and witness, there are compelling reasons to do everything we can to nurture kindness, goodness and connection. I believe that we can maintain continuing bonds with people who have died through love projects that honour their particular legacy.

The kind of projects I have in mind feed into the world based on the intention to keep a cherished person alive in people's hearts. At the same time they help us find our way together.

Glenda's influence on urban food projects in Melbourne was legendary. Some months after her death, when people felt more accepting, we held a walk.

Death: a love project

Colleagues and friends spoke at chosen landmarks about her influence on local councils, organisations like 10,000 Acres and Cultivating Communities, and the people she met. We walked the length of Collingwood and talked about her life, death and the future of her gardening legacy.

> Wendy Whitely speaks of gardening as 'a great lesson in what you can't control'. Deep in grief, soon after her husband Brett's death in 1992, she began clearing the harbourside site of what is now Wendy's Secret Garden in Sydney's Lavender Bay. The Bangalow palms in the heart of the garden were given to her by her daughter, who later died of adrenal cancer. Today, the garden is much visited and dearly loved. It is one of the loveliest public gardens in Sydney. Many weddings and important life events have taken place there. This is a love project.
>
> Well-loved cartoonist Ron Tandberg's final book of pocket cartoons, *A Year of Madness*, was launched some months after his death. He had worked on it with his friend Michael Wilkinson through the later stages of his illness, and was very proud of it. The launch of the book brought friends together again and gave everyone the chance to celebrate his legacy. This is a love project.
>
> Merlene, a client of Karuna Hospice Service, had a very comfortable end to her life. Her family was so impressed by Karuna's outstanding professional service that they

Imaginative visions

wanted to give back. 'What better way to do that than to give them Mum's brand-new car,' said her son of their decision to donate it to the service. This is a love project.

When Hannah – full of life, youth and vitality – died suddenly, her parents and their community put on a vigil and funeral that supported everyone to be together, including many young people who had never lost a friend before. They saw Hannah, looking as they had known her, but not alive as they had known her. They shovelled soil into her grave. This is a love project.

The Age has a weekend column by Barefoot Investor, Scott Pape. People regularly seek his advice on how to invest money they have inherited. He always suggests putting aside some of the money to do something that honours the benefactor. This is a love project.

At 72, Tony knew he only had months to live. He had no fear of being the centre of attention. He held his wake at a time that he could be present, and it drew over 300 people to Byron Bay Golf Club. Titled 'The Awakening', there were five speakers, a ten-piece soul band and all sorts of other entertainments. Tony loved his community – in the end he raised $53,000 through his wake. This was perhaps the biggest ever injection of funds into the local community sector. This is a love project.

Fran and her partner Tova visited India year after year to work on a project cleaning the River Ganga. Fran had colourful shirts made by a tailor who anticipated her visits, picked up the fabrics she'd brought from San Francisco one by one and gave her his opinion of them. After Fran died, her family made the shirts into tea cosies and gave them as gifts. This is a love project.

ALTERNATIVE MEMORIALS

In the funeral industry, memorials are headstones, bronze plaques or lovely vessels to hold ashes. This is fine, but for imaginative and wholehearted people, wonderful visions, actions and decisions can arise from a life's legacy. By spending a little time on changing the ways we meet end of life, we can fulfil larger visions.

The AIDS Memorial Quilt project stands out as a collective recollection of life and death. These massive quilts were created in response to the HIV/AIDS crisis of the 1980s, which took many young lives in a very short time. Elizabeth Taylor spoke of it as 'a rare and intense experience of what it means to be human'.

I saw the AIDS Memorial Quilt panels in Sydney's Domain in the summer of 1992. Traditional communal quilting rituals had been used in a massive healing expression. Sewn on to each panel, in hundreds of different ways, was a life story told in applique and embroidery. Lovers, family members and friends had got together over the project. The quilts seemed to cover an

Imaginative visions

acre of lawn. Brightly coloured four-metre squares, each one made up of quilted pieces, were placed on a grid with wide walkways in-between. Visitors paused to read the stories of people we had never met.

Paul Rohrer: 'Last night it did not seem as if today it would be raining'.
'Nick was my neighbor. He liked art. He was a computer programmer ... He was a great cook.
He was a loner. He never said he was sick.'

Amazing lives and extreme sorrows were recorded and made visible, and I was alive in the middle of them under a blue Sydney sky. It was so sad, and yet the world became a magical place.

The AIDS Memorial Quilt project sprang from an intention to challenge the idea that we should turn away from illness and death. It brought people together across cities and countries around memories, stories, healing and the loss. This is a communal love project.

MAKING LOVE OF LIFE VISIBLE

My vision is that love projects will gain a more visible place at the end of life. Nothing can alter the fact that losing someone we love is sad, often for a long time. But by attending to the demands of death slightly differently, and coming together to appreciate the legacy of a life, it is possible to make a difference to lives in future. By not feeling we have to forget and get on with it, we can engage with the mystery of life. 'How is it that I'm here right now, yet one day in the future I won't be?'

Through the experience of death, we discover a new level of seriousness. We appreciate our lives and create benefits for others through sharing in our sorrow, joy, stories and nurturing intentions. Even at the end of a long period of uncertainty and sadness, a life can make a difference for some time to come – even beyond that into the unforeseeable future.

Resources

ONLINE

- Advance Care Planning Australia
  www.advancecareplanning.org.au
- Kids' Grief Canada, kidsgrief.ca
- 'What should you tell children about death?',
  www.dyingmatters.org
- Death Cafe
  www.deathcafe.org
- The GroundSwell Project
  www.groundswellproject.com
- Funeral Consumers Alliance
  www.fca.org
- National Home Funeral Alliance
  www.nhfa.org
- Australian Doula College
  www.australiandoulacollege.com.au
- For legal advice, go to the website of your state's health department.

BOOKS

- Georgia Blain, *Between a wolf and a dog*, Scribe, 2016
- Ru Callender (ed), *Natural death handbook*, Natural Death Centre, 2009
- Enza Gandolfo, *The bridge*, Scribe, 2018
- Atul Gawande, *Being mortal, medicine and what matters in the end*, Metropolitan Books, 2014
- Kent Haruf, *Our souls at night*, Knopf, 2015
- Susan Minot, *Evening*, Vintage, 1998
- Tillie Olsen and Leo Tolstoy, *The riddle of life and death*, Feminist Press, 2007
- Frank Ostaseski, *The five invitations: discovering what death can teach us about living fully*, Pan Macmillan, 2017
- Holly Stevens, *Undertaken with love: a home funeral guide for families and community care groups*, National Home Funeral Alliance, 2016
- Cory Taylor, *Dying: a memoir*, Scribe, 2016

PODCASTS

- Good Mourning (Australia)
- Centre for Death and Society (UK)
- Let's not be kidding (Canada)
- The Order of the Good Death (US)
- A Path Home (US)

www.ingramcontent.com/pod-product-compliance
Lightning Source LLC
Chambersburg PA
CBHW022017290426
44109CB00015B/1199